Building a Knowledge Base in Reading

Jane Braunger, Ed.D.,
Northwest Regional Educational Laboratory

Jan Patricia Lewis, Ph.D.,
Pacific Lutheran University

Second edition, March 1998

Copublished by:

 Northwest Regional
Educational Laboratory's
Curriculum and Instruction Services
101 S.W. Main Street, Suite 500
Portland, Oregon 97204-3297
(503) 275-9500

 National Council of Teachers of English
1111 W. Kenyon Road, Urbana, IL 61801-1096
Telephone: 800-369-6283 or 217-328-3870
Web: http://www.ncte.org Fax: 217-328-9645

INTERNATIONAL
 Reading Association
800 Barksdale Road, PO Box 8139
Newark, DE 19714-8139, USA (302) 731-1600

Table of Contents

Table of Contents

Introduction

Statement of Purpose

This paper is intended to provide a research baseline for teachers, policymakers, decisionmakers and other interested persons to consider in helping all children meet today's higher literacy standards. At the national, state, and local level, school reform efforts have raised expectations for what readers know and are able to do. At the same time, public awareness of the critical need for proficient reading has been heightened. In this context, it is important for concerned parties to develop shared understandings about the reading process; relationships among skills, strategies, and meaning; and instructional experiences and settings that foster solid reading achievement. Research findings in all of these areas offer an excellent basis for dialogue and planning to bring all students to high levels of literacy.

Throughout the paper, the terms literacy and reading are used interchangeably. The close connections among reading, writing, speaking, and listening are well documented, and current standards incorporate all aspects of literate behavior. Research in the field may focus on one mode of literacy development—for example, reading—but an important lesson of recent research in reading has been that all forms of language and literacy develop supportively and interactively. Children build upon oral language knowledge and strategies as they learn to read and write; they develop key understandings about reading —especially phonics—through writing, and they extend their writing range through reading.

A Higher Stakes Literacy

> Speaking and listening come first. But learning to *read* is, without question, the top priority in elementary education. (Boyer, 1995, p. 69)

So important is learning to read, Boyer continues, that the success of an elementary school is judged by its students' proficiency in reading. In fact, early reading achievement is a very reliable predictor of later school success. Language is essential to learning, and reading, as a specialized form of language, is not only a basic skill, it is an indispensable tool for critical and creative thinking. Literacy allows us to make connections between our own and others' experiences, to inquire systematically into important matters, to access, analyze, and evaluate information and arguments. In short, literacy is key to success in school and beyond, for effective participation in the workforce, the community, and the body politic. This was true in the past—even more true in the future.

But what does it mean to be literate in our society today? In America, the definition of literacy has steadily evolved to suit the increasing demands of our personal, social, economic, and civic lives. Miles Myers (1996) traces this process through specific literacy periods in the United States, each with a different operational definition of literacy. "Signature literacy," the ability to read and write one's name, was the mark of a literate person at the time of our revolution. By the mid 19th century, "recitation literacy" held sway, demonstrated by oral recitation of memorized texts, such as Bible verses. Then in the early 20th century, a higher standard of literacy—the ability to read previously unseen text—resulted from the need to bring many more people, including a large number of immigrants, into productive employment

1

and citizenship. This "decoding/analytic literacy" placed a high priority on decoding individual words and comprehending the literal text. As a definition of literacy it persisted well into the 1980s, and by all accounts our schools have succeeded in teaching this type of literacy, roughly equivalent to the basic reading achievement level of the National Assessment of Educational Progress (NAEP).

Today, more students achieve the basic level on the NAEP than at any other time in our nation's history: On the 1994 NAEP, the achievement at the basic level ranged from 60 percent among fourth-graders to 75 percent among twelfth-graders. At the same time, it must be noted, that only 30 percent of students scored at the "proficient level" and that the number of students who achieve the "advanced" literacy level has barely changed during the 25 years of the test's administration: a mere 7 percent for fourth-graders and 4 percent for twelfth-graders (National Center for Education Statistics, 1995; Allington & Cunningham, 1996).

These numbers should concern us because the literacy demands on students now and in the future are for *proficient* and *advanced*, not merely *basic*, reading ability. To achieve NAEP's *proficient* level, readers "should be able to extend the ideas of the text by making inferences, drawing conclusions, ...making connections to their own personal experiences and other readings, ...[and analyzing] the author's use of literary devices." (Mullis, Campbell, & Farstrup, 1993, pp. 12-17). At the *advanced* level, readers are constructing new understandings by interacting within and across texts, summarizing, analyzing, and evaluating. Advanced readers must be able to use literacy for creative and critical thinking and for problem solving (Pace, 1993). Furthermore, advanced readers consciously apply strategies to text in order to construct meanings from different perspectives and understand how their meanings may differ from those of others (Hiebert, 1991).

Myers calls this higher stakes literacy "critical/translation" literacy; it is the standard which will be required of 21st century "knowledge workers," now learning to read in our schools (Green & Dixon, 1996). And yet, it is estimated that only about 15 percent of our students are achieving this level of literacy (Allington & Cunningham, 1996).

In our society, the movement from an industrial to a knowledge era has influenced our thinking about learning as well as literacy. While basic skills are essential components of literacy, reasoning and critical thinking are increasingly important. The knowledge base, once thought to be fixed, is evolving, so ongoing learning is essential. Finally, while individual achievement and independence continue to be valued outcomes of schooling, collaboration is increasingly understood to be necessary for success in learning as in other endeavors (Roehler, 1997).

The Present Problem: Bringing More Students to Higher Literacy Levels

Clearly, the standards for literacy are higher than they have ever been. Productive functioning in our society will require higher levels of literacy than in previous eras and these higher levels will be required of a larger percentage of the population. At the same time, increasing numbers of children are entering school who are likely to experience difficulty learning to read (Graves, Van den Broek, & Taylor, 1996). Overwhelmingly, it is poor and minority children who fail to succeed as readers, and their numbers are growing in our schools. In Washington state, for example, the ethnic and cultural population is increasing at a faster rate than the White population. From 1980-1990 increases of 30 percent (Asian), 26 percent (Hispanic), and 13 percent (Black) contrasted to 4 percent growth among the White population. The state's largest group of English language learners are Spanish speaking. In 1995, 5.7 percent of Washington's population was Hispanic; by 2005, it is expected to rise to 7.2 percent.[1] A consequence of this trend for schools is an ever-growing population of minority children, now concentrated in the primary grades.

It should be noted that children who are members of ethnic and cultural minorities and/or poor do not by definition experience difficulty in learning to read. However, these are the groups with whom public schools have had the least success overall in achieving high levels of literacy. The foregoing indicators of growth in these populations are offered mainly to emphasize the urgency of ensuring success in reading for all children.

Long before they come to school, children are building on their experiences and their oral language to become strategic thinkers and readers in a process known as emergent literacy. We already know that children raised in safe, nurturing, and stimulating environments are better learners than those raised in less stimulating settings and that the cognitive and affective effects can be long lasting (Carnegie Corporation, 1994). Recent research also points to the importance of language exposure and experience to children's vocabulary growth and cognitive development (Hart & Risley, 1995). Well before the age of three, children are on a trajectory of language development in which "the amount and diversity of their past experience influences which new opportunities for experience they notice and choose" (p. 194). Poor children are at a distinct disadvantage for amount and richness of language interactions which stimulate cognitive development. The consequences for their success in school, specifically learning to read confidently and critically, are alarming. Too many children move into the intermediate grades without control of reading skills and strategies necessary for effective, satisfying uses of literacy. Yet, as tenacious as the reading problem is, we know more than we ever did about the reading process and about how to teach reading. Steady gains in the basic reading abilities of students in the lowest performing groups have been documented over the 25 years of the NAEP reading assessment (Graves, Van den Broek, & Taylor, 1996). The performance gap between privileged, middle-class students and poor, minority students is closing, but it is still too wide. As P. David Pearson (1996) points out, "as a profession we seem most able to provide help to those students who need it least and, conversely, least able to provide help to those who need it most" (p. 304).

To address this problem, it is important to examine the fit between reading instruction and the new, higher standards of literacy. Instruction in literal comprehension, locating and remembering details, pronouncing words, and answering factual questions is appropriate to teach basic reading or the decoding/analytical literacy Myers describes. However, such an approach is inadequate to ensure that all children develop more advanced, critical/ translation literacy.

Pearson (1996) emphasizes that there is no magic potion, no silver bullet, to ensure that all children will develop the literacy skills they need to function effectively in today's society. There are no easy solutions, so it is all the more important that teachers have vast knowledge to apply to the design of instruction. He states, "They need to understand language, literacy,

---

[1] Statistics from the Office of the Superintendent of Public Instruction, Olympia, Washington, 1997.

and learning well enough to adapt teaching and learning environments, materials, and methods to particular situations, groups, and individuals" (p. 304). The Carnegie Task Force on Learning in the Primary Grades (1996) adds that teachers must continually enhance their own knowledge to ensure children's success; higher standards for learning demand this.

Part of this required knowledge is how sociocultural and linguistic variables affect learning to read. Teachers need to understand the uses and values of literacy in the many cultures from which children in any classroom may come. For children whose first language is not English, the process requires that many variables be addressed. Such factors as literacy in the first language, health issues for immigrants, the decision of whether to teach literacy in the first or in the second language (English), world view and background experiences and knowledge, and schooling experiences in the home country are crucial to effective acquisition of literacy. The makeup of public schools today does not support a "one size fits all" program of reading instruction; rather, teachers must be able to provide instruction appropriate to the diversity of children's experiences and needs.

Furthermore, teachers must recognize and work to eliminate the ways in which students' ethnicity, culture, language, and social class are used by schools, consciously or unconsciously, as an explanation for students' success or failure (Nieto, 1997). For students learning to speak and to read in English, issues of intergroup hostility, subordinate status of a minority group, cultural stereotyping, and patterns of acculturation versus assimilation have a profound effect on their acquisition of English and their success in school (Collier, 1995).

Obviously, the challenge to public schools to bring all children to high levels of literacy function is unprecedented and complex. The task is made even more daunting by a lack of public consensus on (a) a definition of reading and (b) the relevant knowledge base to inform primary reading instruction.

In this paper, we attempt to fashion such a consensus by detailing what is known about how children learn to read and the environments that support the process. We have identified 13 core understandings about reading that knowledgeable teachers have, understandings informed by various research traditions and demonstrated by the classroom environments such teachers design. As teachers, parents, and policymakers act in their respective roles on these understandings, all children can be supported to develop the sophisticated literacy skills required for personal, social, civic, and economic fulfillment.

Core Understandings About Learning to Read

The understandings listed here will be explained in detail in a later section of the paper. The first four flow from the nature of reading as language; it is always about meaning and communication. The remaining points address the fact that reading is a learned, rather than an acquired, language behavior, dependent on mastering a written code based on the alphabetic principle. Allington and Cunningham sum up the essential tension, "Reading and writing are meaning constructing activities, but they are dependent on words" (1996, p. 49).

1. Reading is a construction of meaning from written text. It is an active, cognitive, and affective process.

2. Background knowledge and prior experience are critical to the reading process.

3. Social interaction is essential in learning to read.

4. Reading and writing develop together.

5. Reading involves complex thinking.

6. Environments rich in literacy experiences, resources, and models facilitate reading development.

7. Engagement in the reading task is key in successfully learning to read.

8. Children's understandings of print are not the same as adults' understandings.

9. Children develop phonemic awareness and knowledge of phonics through a variety of literacy opportunities, models, and demonstrations.

10. Children learn successful reading strategies in the context of real reading.

11. Children learn best when teachers employ a variety of strategies to model and demonstrate reading knowledge, strategy, and skills.

12. Children need the opportunity to read, read, read.

13. Monitoring the development of reading processes is vital to student success.

Defining Reading

Our definition of reading leads inevitably to the way we teach children to read. Listed below are excerpts that show how current definitions emphasize movement beyond basic skills and how national and state standards reflect this notion of reading as a complex, interactive process, using basic skills and advanced strategies to make meaning:

- The National Literacy Act of 1991 defines literacy as "an individual's ability to read, write, and speak in English and compute and solve problems at levels of proficiency necessary to function on the job and in society to achieve one's goals, and to develop one's knowledge and potential" (IRA/NCTE, 1996, p. 4).

- Being literate in contemporary society means being active, critical, and creative users not only of print and spoken language but also of the visual language of film and television, commercial and political advertising, photography, and more (IRA/NCTE 1996, p. 5).

- "I define reading as a message-getting, problem-solving activity which increases in power and flexibility the more it is practiced. My definition states that within the directional constraints of the printer's code, language and visual perception responses are purposefully directed by the reader in some integrated way to the problem of extracting meaning from cues in a text, in sequence, so that the reader brings a maximum of understanding to the author's message" (Clay, 1991, p. 6).

- There has been a well-documented shift from a literal, decoding model of reading to one of reading as a strategic process in which readers construct meaning by interacting with text. They use not only what is in the text—words and their meanings—but what they bring to the text—their own knowledge and experiences to construct meaning. In addition, the interactions among teacher and students, the purposes for reading, and the context within which the literacy events occur all affect the construction of meaning and the development of reading strategies (Sweet, 1993, p. 1).

- "Reading is not merely a skill; it is an engagement of the person in a conceptual and social world" (Guthrie, 1997, p. 3). New research shows engagement as essential to achievement in reading (Allen, Michalove, & Shockley, 1993; Baker, Afflerbach, & Reinking, 1996; Shockley, Michalove, & Allen, 1995). Engaged readers are strategic, knowledgeable, motivated, and social in their approach to learning and using literacy (Morrow, 1996). These engagements are vital because they start "a positive spiral of reading, knowing, and sharing" (Guthrie, 1997, p. 3).

- Reading is "the process of constructing meaning through the dynamic interaction among the reader's existing knowledge, the information suggested by the written language, and the context of the reading situation" (Michigan Department of Education, 1989). The state of Washington incorporated this definition in its Essential Academic Learning Requirements (EALRs) for reading.

- In Washington state, The Framework for Achieving the Essential Academic Learning Requirements in Reading, The Assessments of Student Learning in Reading, and the Leadership in Reading staff development project all reflect a model of reading as a process. Washington's Essential Academic Learnings in Reading call for students to (a) understand and use a variety of strategies to read, (b) understand the meaning of what is read, (c) read different materials for a variety of purposes, and (d) set goals and evaluate progress to improve reading. It is important to note that the document defines "understands the meaning of what is read" to include analysis, interpretation, synthesis, and critical thinking about text (Commission on Student Learning, 1996).

From Definition to Instruction

The evidence for a high-stakes, complex view of literacy today is abundant. And yet a debate about the teaching of reading continues, partly because of public concern over some students' low achievement in reading. However, another serious problem fuels the debate, namely the lack of a public consensus on what we mean by reading. Connie Weaver, a prominent literacy educator, suggests that this disagreement rests on three conflicting views of what it means to learn to read:

> View 1: Learning to read means learning to pronounce words.

View 2: Learning to read means learning to identify words and get their meaning.

View 3: Learning to read means learning to bring meaning *to* a text in order to get meaning *from* it (Weaver, 1994, p. 15).

In fact, these views are not exclusive; each one contains and progresses beyond the previous one, in effect bringing together the changing views of literacy. This is similar to the process described earlier in which each new definition of literacy in the United States subsumed the old ones and raised the standard. Still, to some extent debates about reading instruction today reflect primary allegiance to different views of reading. What we know about reading as a language function is that it is always about meaning; sounding out words is necessary but not sufficient to the task. In ESL teaching, there is the added issue of transferability of reading skills learned in the home language to reading in English. This question parallels the debate for mainstream learners about teaching isolated skills versus skills embedded in meaningful encounters with text.

Still, as we think about preparing children to be literate at the levels required for the 21st century, it is important to see that unlocking the code and reading the words is only a part of the complex, socially constructed, and cognitively demanding process called reading.

Recently, the International Reading Association (IRA) published a position statement, *The Role of Phonics in Reading Instruction*, to make that very point. IRA supports a view of reading as "the complex process of understanding written texts." The statement affirms that phonics is an essential aspect of beginning reading instruction, one that teachers do value and teach. However, the document expresses concerns with inaccurate claims and distortions about the role of phonics in beginning reading. The statement concludes,

> . . .exaggerated claims of the failure of students in learning to read serve only to divert our attention, energies, and resources from the important issues we must face. Explanations that focus on simple solutions like more phonics instruction are misguided. The problems we face [in ensuring that all children learn to read] are complex and require inquiring minds (IRA, January, 1997).

Indeed, learning to read and write is a complex activity. What is needed to ensure that all children acquire reading and writing proficiency is a balanced instructional effort that incorporates the strengths of different classroom literacy approaches—from phonics to trade books—and applies what we know about how children learn to be literate (Allington & Cunningham, 1996).

What Counts as Knowledge About Beginning Reading?

Over the past 50 years, there has been more research focused on language arts, on reading and writing, than ever before (Purcell-Gates, 1997). We have come to understand that reading, in and out of school, is part of a much larger, more complex array of making sense of the world around us. Further, we have come to appreciate how a variety of disciplines and research traditions informs us about how children learn to read. The lenses of different research traditions have helped us see a fuller picture of reading. Cognitive psychology, educational anthropology, linguistics, and sociology have all contributed to the knowledge base about reading, its acquisition, and its processes (Pearson & Stephens, 1994). Research in language acquisition and emergent literacy has provided especially rich insights into our knowledge of reading. In addition to their findings, these various traditions have offered more effective research methods for getting at what readers know and can do. As a result, we have been able to frame new questions for study in understanding the reading process; not only our knowledge base, but also our scope of inquiry has grown.

Research on the brain, for example, has shown the enormous impact on later learning of children's early experiences with language and exposure to the world (Carnegie Corporation, 1994; Hart & Risley, 1995; Healy, 1990). Research on miscue analysis has helped us understand children's reading errors in the context of their attempt to construct meaning with text (K. Goodman, 1965; Y. Goodman, 1976). Research on the engagement perspective has offered insights into motivation, self-monitoring, and independent use of reading strategies (Morrow, 1996). And research on emergent literacy has shown us the importance of home and community literacy practices to children's success in learning to read and write in school (Purcell-Gates, 1997).

In addition, research on adult literacy has yielded valuable insights for young children's development as readers. Adults need real-world applications of literacy that build upon current knowledge (Sticht, Caylor, Kern & Fox, 1972), and they need to use literacy to accomplish their own purposes (Freire, 1970). These findings are relevant to children as well and have been incorporated into many classrooms' literacy designs.

Still, a lack of consensus about the definition of reading is played out in disagreements not only about how best to teach reading, but also about what counts as knowledge about how children learn to read. A true definition of reading must include both decoding and constructing meaning, but the current reading wars have often had the unfortunate effect of wrenching apart these two essential components of reading. Yvonne and David Freeman (personal communication, 1997) describe how contrasting definitions of reading as recoding (decoding) and reading as meaning construction lead to disagreements about knowledge base and instruction.

If one believes that decoding is the major task in learning to read, it follows that children are successful to the extent they learn to decode print accurately. Likewise, what counts as professional knowledge is evidence of how and to what degree children learn to pronounce words on the page. Knowledge about reading development in this view comes from empirical studies with control and experimental groups; testing in these studies is typically standardized tests of letter/sound knowledge, word knowledge in isolation, and accuracy of oral reading. Such tests provide valuable information about a student's reading achievement; however, they leave out important contextual factors of the reading process and of engagement, to note just two. Much of the current public interest in how and when children learn—or can be taught— phonemic awareness (Adams, 1990) may stem from a misperception of reading as solely decoding. The IRA's recent (1997) statement on phonics raised issues about the role of phonics in learning to read. Further, it soundly criticized contributions of the press and popular media to inadequate representations of reading.

On the other hand, if one sees reading as a process of constructing meaning, then evidence of growth in reading will include many indicators from numerous sources, including but not limited to achievement test data. Additional evidence of children's literacy development comes from naturalistic studies of children actually reading, for example, teachers' observations and analysis of literacy learning experiences; classroom research on the impact of social interaction, strategic modeling, and literacy materials on literacy learning; children's use of all the cueing systems in reading (letter/sound, meaning, syntax, and pragmatics); connections between children's reading and writing; and a host of other variables involved in the reading process. In this view, the test of children's achievement as readers is based on observation of them reading complete texts, and on data collection with tools such as miscue analysis and retellings. Instruction always moves from whole to part; the text is a meaningful whole, whose parts, e.g., structures and words, can be looked at in that context.

Questions about research. The engagement perspective described earlier has implications for conducting research on reading. It suggests that frequent problems in using research to inform teaching practice are due to the fact that so much research-based knowledge is not drawn from actual classroom settings. When experimental studies control out factors, the findings don't map well onto the messy, real-world classrooms of teachers who might want to apply the lessons of research to improve students' learning. Current brain research suggests that a more important issue may be the limitations of rational/experimental research for studying the complex processes in reading as meaning-making (Caine & Caine, 1991). Placing research into context has led to qualitative research strategies, e.g., case studies and participant observation, as well as quantitative research strategies, e.g., quasi-experiments and causal modeling, that keep contextual factors together in the classroom (Guthrie, 1997).

A debate has continued for some time between empirical researchers who criticize qualitative research on literacy learning and others who embrace interpretive scholarship in the field, (Anderson & West, 1995; Edelsky, 1990; Eisenhart, 1995; McKenna, Robinson, & Miller, 1990; Myers, 1995). Critics of interpretivist research accuse it of having no standards or applying them inconsistently. However, Peter Mosenthal (1995) suggests that the division in the research community goes beyond what standards should apply; the issue is how to develop consensus about what should be "the collective literacy agenda for all" (p. 577).

Reaching consensus on a literacy agenda, as Mosenthal suggests, would probably yield rich studies of both sorts, but it would take a thoughtful, respectful dialogue about current understandings of literacy. More research seems needed in the social, cultural, and political issues in literacy instruction. Research from the learner's perspective that looks at meanings and values for literacy in the home culture is increasing, but we need more.

Large-scale generalizations for policy and insights for classroom teaching may emerge from either quantitative or qualitative research. The discussion of what counts as knowledge about how children learn to read goes beyond the relative merits of quantitative and qualitative research. In fact, most literacy researchers see the value in both for different lines of inquiry and application to literacy learning. So it is important that teachers know how to read, evaluate, and apply the findings emerging from both research approaches.

For this discussion, a point to be made about the value of qualitative research is that it takes into consideration the context of the activity being studied (reading), often through participant observation. The presumed loss of objectivity (highly valued in quantitative research) can actually benefit a teacher of reading. As Glesne and Peshkin (1992) point out, "The more you function as a member of the everyday world of the researched, the more you risk losing the eye of the uninvolved outsider; yet, the more you participate, *the greater your opportunity to learn*" (p. 40, italics added). For teachers researching their own classrooms, Lytle and Cochran-Smith (1992) note that "systematic subjectivity" is essential.

The importance of practitioner knowledge. In this paper, we have cast a broad, cross-disciplinary net to capture knowledge about how children learn to read. One important knowledge source is teachers themselves. It is important to understand how teachers develop knowledge about beginning reading. They do this through their own formal education, their reading and reflecting on the work of published researchers, their close observation of and reflection on children reading in their classrooms, their sharing of classroom-based insights with each other, and their ongoing study of their classrooms in light of new understandings from teachers' and researchers' work.

Teachers' classroom studies provide invaluable knowledge about reading. Through their classroom research, teachers develop personal theories and use their practical knowledge and theoretical expertise. They recognize themselves and are recognized by others as professionals in the classrooms, schools, and communities (Taylor, 1993). In addition, teachers design curriculum, either alone or with others, based on their research, and they adjust their practice based on their conclusions from the study (Patterson & Shannon in Patterson, Santa, Short, & Smith (eds.), 1993). Research by teachers into children's learning in their own classrooms is "a distinctive and important way of knowing about teaching" (Taylor, 1993, p. 129). Knowledge about how children learn to read, what helps and hinders the process, must include teachers' knowledge obtained by such close observation, reflection, and analysis.

The impact of teacher research on what we know and how we teach literacy is highlighted in a recent article by Shanahan and Neuman (1997). Among the 13 research studies they selected as most affecting literacy instruction since 1965 were Donald Graves' study of children's writing (1981) and Nancy Atwell's study of middle school students' writing and reading (1987). In both these studies, the teachers told their stories of immersing children in authentic reading and writing tasks, and through their reflections on daily classroom life, drew a map for other teachers/travelers to follow in making their classrooms places where children become readers and writers.

These teacher-researchers took the learner's perspective to discover what makes children want to read and write, how they develop increasing control over literacy processes, and the types of teacher interventions and classroom interactions that supported the process. Taking the learner's perspective turns out to be good advice for researchers as well as for teachers.

Toward a knowledge base about beginning reading. We are fortunate to be asking the question, "How do children learn to read?" at a time when the knowledge base is informed by research from the learner's perspective as well as by more traditional treatment effect studies. Rich studies of literacy development before, during, and outside of school add to our growing knowledge of the process and allow us to identify classroom practices that help, or hinder, children in the process of becoming literate. In this paper, criteria for research contributing to knowledge about reading include (a) evidence of seminal studies, (b) recency, (c) validation of current perspectives or introduction of new perspectives on learning, and (d) application to a broad range of learners.

The remaining sections of this paper summarize key findings from such research on learning to read. Important related areas are explored, including oral language acquisition and connections between oral and written language, culture and literacy, and factors influencing children's literacy development. Finally, the current knowledge base about beginning reading is distilled into 13 core understandings with sample classroom applications.

Acquiring Language: Basic Understandings

How Do We Learn?

Young children are, to say the least, sponges. Current research in the early development of the brain assigns more and more emphasis to the experiences and interactions that occur. Interaction is the key: How those around the child—parents, siblings, caregivers—talk and engage in experiences with the child seems to hold critical importance. Ability is not fixed within each individual, but rather a process where experience and environment are key factors in development of potential. Such research has powerful implications for work with beginning readers.

A study synthesizing research on brain development within the first three years points to five key findings (Carnegie Corporation, 1994):

1. Brain development that takes place before age one is more rapid and extensive than we previously realized.

2. Brain development is much more vulnerable to environmental influence than we ever expected (Hart & Risley, 1995).

3. The influence of early environment on brain development is long lasting.

4. The environment affects not only the number of brain cells and number of connections among them, but also the way these connections are "wired."

5. We have new scientific evidence for the negative impact of early stress on brain function (pp. 7-9).

Work in the cognitive sciences and the neurosciences as well as advances in other fields builds upon these notions. It shows effective learning occurs when these factors are in place: direct engagement of the learner; social process; the learner's purposes and intentions driving the learning; hypothesis testing; and a search for meaning (Caine & Caine, 1991, 1997).

Patterning (maps and categories, both acquired and innate) is emphasized as a critical learning strategy, including emotions as an important aspect. Caine and Caine's research has also found that the brain simultaneously perceives and creates parts and wholes; that is, the brain reduces information into parts and perceives wholistically at the same time. Learning involves both focused attention and peripheral perception; it always involves conscious and unconscious processes. In sum, learning is a complex process, embedded within our social interactions. This is compatible with meaning-centered literacy instruction, that is, instruction that focuses on the construction of meaning (1991, p. 80).

How children learn, be it language or any other knowledge, has long been at the heart of research in psychology, the sciences, and education. Brain research extends and supports this tradition. Currently, most models of how children acquire language knowledge have a foundation based in Piagetian (1969) constructs; that is, children learn via interactions and experiences within their environment. The work of Russian psychologist Vygotsky (1978) adds another critical dimension to children's learning with an emphasis on the importance of *social* interaction. Vygotsky's theories put a focus on the construction of meaning as central: Both personal and social meanings are socially constructed. In contrast to Piaget's theories, language is central to this process rather than reflecting but not determining thought (Pace, 1993).

Vygotsky's work also describes a "zone of proximal development" in children's learning. This is the range of social interaction between a novice and more knowledgeable other in which the child can perform with degrees of assistance from an adult that which s/he cannot yet perform independently. The zone of proximal development ends at the level at which the child can operate independently. These social interactions involve scaffolding—the support needed by the learner—to progress in understanding and ability. Cognitive development is promoted since thought and language processes that begin interpersonally later become intrapersonal (Pace, 1993).

Critical to this evolving view of early language learning is the increasing number of researchers focusing on the child's perspective on learning, rather than focusing on an adult's perspective of what learning ought to be (Dahl & Freppon, 1995; Ferreiro & Teberosky, 1982; Teale, 1982). Research methodologies have emerged that allow a closer view of what children do as they learn, particularly as they learn to speak, listen, write, and read; of their developing understandings of reading; and of how they learn to make sense of the meaning they create. Dahl and Freppon (1995) believe these developments to be particularly important in the context of current debates about differing instructional approaches, particularly for low-income children who are most at risk for failure. It is important to better understand how children view reading and writing behaviors from different perspectives in order to provide instruction and experience that best meet their needs.

In the same way, the teachers in the Webster Grove (Missouri) Action Research Project learned to look closely at interactions between themselves and their students to see ways in which they could better support students in becoming effective writers. Teachers took the learners' perspective to see how to help them capitalize on their strengths as writers (informal voice and personal engagement with their subject). Basically, their study began with a goal of "fixing" the students' writing, and, through their case study research, that goal shifted to "fixing the teaching methods" and finally, "fixing the relationships between teachers and students" (Krater, Zeni, & Cason, 1994).

Clearly, the need for rich language experiences based in everyday experiences is critical to the cognitive and language development of young children. Educators must be aware of this important element and continue to provide rich experiences for children as they begin formal education.

Language Learning: Acquisition and Development

> ...anything that can be said of human language and language learning has some vital bearing upon the processes of literacy. (Holdaway, 1979, p. 13)

Investigation into how children acquire language has grown immensely during the past 40 years. Chomsky's (1959, 1967) notion that all humans actively construct meaning led to questions beyond the long-held behaviorist view of response theory. Chomsky's new perspective and alternative questions have led to a series of investigations that have given increasing insight into how children learn oral language, which, in turn, invites consideration of how children then acquire written language. Because of the relative newness of this area of investigation, consensus remains elusive on many points. Disciplines and subdisciplines interested in such investigations—e.g., cognitive and developmental psychology, psycholinguistics/sociolinguistics/linguistics, anthropology, education—consider questions from such a wide variety of perspectives that difference is found more often than is similarity. These investigations have, however, helped us to gain insight into the processes of acquisition and development of children's language. In general, this research helps us to understand that oral language development is:

- *A process of reconstructing the child's home language through interactions with more sophisticated language users.* Language learning is much more than simple imitation; rather, it is a complex process of trial and error through approximations. Learning language is an intellectual, cognitive process (R. Brown, 1973; R. Brown, Cazden, & Bellugi-Klima, 1968; Halliday, 1975; Piaget & Inhelder, 1969).

- *Meaning based.* Language has a purpose: to communicate needs, wants, feelings. Halliday (1975) suggests learning language is "learning how to mean" in one's culture. Children will take on a language form because of its function—initially understanding the function, and through use, becoming clear about the form itself.

- *Social.* Language is for communication among people, and it is acquired through purposeful and meaningful interactions (Bruner, 1975; Harste, Woodward, & Burke, 1984; Neuman & Roskos, 1993; Vygotsky, 1978; Wells, 1986).

- *Interactive.* Children learn language via scaffolds provided by sophisticated language users; that is, they offer opportunities for children to try out approximations and through constructive and positive feedback, assist children toward gaining conventions of the language (Applebee & Langer, 1983; Bruner, 1975; Cambourne, 1988; Vygotsky, 1978; Wells, 1986).

- *Developmental.* Children's language acquisition occurs in stages that are documentable. Often, children's processes of hypothesis generation (i.e., figuring out how language works) are demonstrated through their language "errors" (R. Brown, 1973; Wells, 1986).

- *In a dynamic relationship with listening, reading, and writing: Each influences the other in the course of development.* Brown and Cambourne (1990), elaborating on a visual metaphor designed by Harste, Burke and Woodward (1983), describe this relationship in terms of a "linguistic data pool"; this means that all language learners have an ever-increasing pool of knowledge about language, and are continually adding to it whether reading, writing, listening, or speaking (p. 24).

Language as function. It is important to consider Halliday's (1975, pp. 19-21; cf. Pinnell, 1985) notion that language is functional. According to his theory of developmental language, what a child can do during interactions with others has meaning and meaning can be turned into speech: What can be said reflects what can be done. In his work, he describes the following functions of language:

    Instrumental: language to satisfy a personal need and to get things done

    Regulatory: language to control the behavior of others

    Interactional: language to get along with others

    Personal: language to tell about oneself

    Imaginative: language to pretend, to make believe

    Heuristic: language to find out about things, to learn things

    Informative: language to communicate something for the information of others

Children's acquisition of oral language does seem to follow a pattern: Children seem to be more interested in the functions of literacy first, then the form, and later the conventions (Halliday, 1973, 1975; cf. Morrow, 1996, p. 141).

A model of acquisition. Based on a synthesis of Halliday's (and others') work and his own investigations, Cambourne (1988, pp. 28-75) provides a useful model of conditions that support successful oral language learning:

- *Immersion.* From birth we are immersed in the language of our culture. Learners need to be immersed in all kinds of language.

- *Demonstration.* Learners need to receive many demonstrations of how language is constructed and used.

- *Engagement.* Deep engagement with demonstrations is maximized when learners are convinced that (a) they are potential doers of whatever is being demonstrated; (b) engaging with what is being demonstrated will further the purposes of the potential learners' lives; (c) engagement with whatever is being demonstrated will not lead to pain, humiliation, denigration—it is safe to have a go at it. In addition, learners are more likely to engage with the demonstrations provided by those who are significant to them.

- *Expectation.* Expectations of those to whom learners are bonded send clear messages to children as to what they are expected to learn AND what they are capable of learning. Learners respond positively and confidently to supportive expectations.

- *Responsibility.* Learners need to participate in making decisions about when, how, and what bits to learn in any learning task.

- *Approximation.* Learners must be free to approximate the desired model—mistakes are essential for learning to occur.

- *Use.* Learners need time and opportunity to use, employ, and practice their developing control in functional, realistic, nonartificial ways.

- *Response.* Learners must receive feedback from exchanges with more knowledgeable others. Response must be relevant, appropriate, timely, readily available, nonthreatening, with no strings attached.

Connections between oral language and the "language of print." Cambourne (1988) believes these conditions also support the learning of written language. While there is much debate over the parallels between the learning of oral language and the learning of print (reading and writing), it is important to note both the similarities and the differences, and how these apply to acquisition and development.

Similarities. Reading, writing, speaking, and listening, at the deep levels of production and comprehension, are parallel manifestations of the same vital human function—the mind's effort to create meaning (Cambourne, 1988, p. 29). Cognitively, the same processes seem to be in effect with all language processes. Children go through developmental stages in ways similar to oral language development.

Differences. The two modes of language differ in many complex and interesting ways. These differences are due to such pragmatic factors as psychological and physical distance from audience, function, amount of time people have to produce language, and degree of permanence (Chafe & Danielewicz, 1986; Olson, 1977; Rubin, 1978; Tannen, 1982). Most obviously, the two require different kinds of knowledge which learners must acquire in order to operate with and on them. And, of course, there are certain aspects of the use of the written mode that require specific knowledge which can't be carried over from the oral mode and vice versa. Cambourne (1988) discusses these differences in detail.

- Written language is not merely oral language which has been written down. For example, it is used for quite different purposes, in quite different contexts, under quite different conditions.

- The same privileges for learning the written mode are not as available as those for the oral. That is, while oral language is constantly surrounding us in a variety of means (personal, recorded, and so on), print language must be created and made accessible. Someone must construct a text—a newspaper, a letter, a list, a sign, a billboard—and make it available for others to read. Classrooms must provide a wide variety of opportunities to access print—through books, charts, lists, labels—so that children have opportunities to interact with them in real and meaningful ways parallel to oral language (cf. Cambourne, pp. 29, 43-45).

Moustafa (1997) suggests that children need to learn the language of print, that is, based upon their knowledge of oral language, they need to learn how the language of print works. Just as with oral language, children are figuring out how print works concurrently with learning to read (reminiscent of Halliday's learning through language and about language while learning language). Clay (1972) similarly speaks of children's "concepts about print"; that is, they understand the concepts of a book, of how to turn the pages, read from left to right, that meaning comes from print and pictures, and so on. Most importantly, children understand the concept that reading is for enjoyment and for information—it is purposeful and functional in their lives. These must be learned through scaffolded experiences specifically with print. Wells (1986) points out that reading to children also helps them acquire the language of print. The work of Mason (1992), Sulzby (1985), and Purcell-Gates (1988) also supports the importance of reading aloud to children. These experiences give children a sense of the language of print, putting them in an even better position to figure out print on their own (Moustafa, 1997).

Cambourne's (1988) work suggests this learning must be supported by the same conditions as oral language. In fact, Cambourne goes further, saying that his model of language learning reflects how humans go about learning in general. His conditions for learning language reflect basic principles that can guide effective teaching and learning of language. Thus, experiences in and out of schools must be provided by teachers and parents to assist children in their development (pp. 40-42).

Emergent Literacy

Traditionally, adults viewed a discrete set of skills deemed necessary for children to begin to read as "readiness." Typically, this included knowledge of colors, shapes, and the alphabet. The notion of emergent literacy—coined by Marie Clay (1966)—turned the focus from this adult idea of readiness to what children acquired from their surrounding environments that provides a foundation for beginning literacy. Research across cultures has provided substance to the idea of emergent literacy. These researchers have focused explicitly upon how children go about their learning, rather than upon a set of tasks configured by adults to represent the learning. In a very general sense, emergent literacy describes those behaviors shown by very young children as they begin to respond to and approximate reading and writing acts. By the time children enter first grade, they are often ready to move into more sophisticated behaviors. However, development varies. Ferreiro and Teberosky (1982); Harste, Woodward and Burke (1984); Heath (1983); Morrow (1978, 1997); Sulzby (1985); Taylor (1983); Teale (1982, 1986); and Wells (1986) provide insight into how young children use the same type of learning strategies seen in oral language to begin to make sense of the print they find in their world. Generally, children:

- *Have gained oral language structures*: syntax (structure) and meaning, in particular. In oral language, they have begun to experiment with the sounds language makes. This understanding and knowledge is an important foundation transferred to learning the language of print.

- *Find meaning in symbols around them*. Early on, signs and symbols (e.g., McDonald's golden arches, labels from familiar products) take on important meaning: The environmental print in children's lives has a real function. These signs and symbols reflect what is available and meaningful within the lives of those around the child, from letters to symbols found in everyday life (Goodman, 1984; Harste, Woodward, & Burke, 1984; Mason, 1980; Smith, 1971).

- *Begin to write, using symbols, signs, and letters in their attempts to reconstruct the symbolic language around them* (Bissex, 1980; Harste, Woodward, & Burke, 1984; Sulzby, 1986).

- *Begin to approximate print behaviors modeled to them*: storybook reading, use of storybook language and behaviors, approximation of writing tasks modeled (lists, stories, etc.). Often, these approximations occur within the child's play (Heath, 1983; Sulzby, 1985; Wells, 1986).

- *Follow a developmental pattern in reading and writing* (Morrow, 1997, p. 141). These patterns reinforce the use and emergence of language cues for the knowledge systems of sound-symbol relationships, meaning, structure, and purpose. The patterns suggest process, and as these processes are repeated they are refined. Language acquisition is not additive; rather, children are repeating the whole process, refining, getting clearer and clearer with time and experience.

- *Begin to categorize speech sounds to print patterns* (Read, 1975). They create their own spelling patterns, based upon their perception of how language works, and how they can fit it together.

Importance of family in emergent literacy. Literacy is deeply embedded in the social processes of family life (Taylor, 1983). Families influence literacy development in three ways (Leichter, 1984): through interpersonal interaction (literacy experiences shared by family members), the physical environment (literacy materials found in the home), and the emotional and motivational climate (the relationships and their attitudes toward literacy). In general, parent involvement in education is directly related to significant increases in overall student achievement (Bloom, 1985; Clark, 1983).

Home and school connections are critical to learning to read. Children who have had a wide variety of language experiences—in both oral and written modes—fare better as they begin to learn to read within the school setting. These experiences include:

- *Many opportunities to talk*: descriptions and conversations with positive interactions and feedback from those around the child (Bruner, 1975; Cazden, 1988; Hart & Risley, 1995; Ninio & Bruner, 1978).

- *Experiences with stories, both oral (storytelling) and written (storybook reading)* (Holdaway, 1979; Sulzby, 1985; Teale, 1978, 1982; Wells, 1986). Storybook reading experiences are considered by many to be the most important aspect of emergent literacy experiences (Purcell-Gates, McIntyre, & Freppon, 1995), giving children the structure and syntax of written language as well as demonstrating purpose and function of reading (Heath, 1982; Morrow, O'Connor, & Smith, 1990; Sulzby, 1985; Taylor & Strickland, 1986). If children do not have this background framework upon which to hang the more explicit literacy experiences received in schools, lack of success can occur.

- *Appropriate verbal interaction between adult and child during story readings* (Cochran Smith, 1984; Ninio, 1980). Edwards (1989, 1991) found that nonmainstream parents can successfully be taught how to interact with books in ways that support successful literacy development.

- *Opportunities to draw and write* (Clay, 1977). Drawing and writing support children's interest in and growing awareness of print in their environment.

Factors that Influence Literacy Learning

Culture and Literacy: What Difference Does Difference Make?

Critical to the successful acquisition of reading is the match between cultural expectations for literacy and school expectations for literacy. These are not always the same, and children's experiences with literacy will vary accordingly. For example, in some cultures storytelling is highly valued over the use of print materials (Morrow, 1996). Families help children to appreciate and understand the social significance of literacy—however it may be defined for individuals (Clay, 1972; Taylor, 1983). However, studies have found the types and forms of literacy practiced in some homes—often of low income, ethnic and cultural minority, and immigrant families—to be largely incongruent with the literacy encountered in school (Heath, 1983; Taylor & Dorsey-Gaines, 1988). This research identifies families as literate in ways defined by their culture and community—for example, cultures rich in oral traditions—rather than in the ways defined by school literacy. These studies challenge assumptions about uniform definitions of literacy as well as about the concern of parents for their children's education (cf. Chavkin, 1989; Comer, 1986; Snow, Barnes, Chandler, Goodman, & Hemphill, 1991).

Since oral language provides the foundation and framework for written language acquisition, a mismatch can cause a lack of success in learning to read within a school situation. With increasing diversity among the population, children come to school with a wide variety of oral language patterns and expectations, as well as a wide variety of experience with print language (Hall, 1987). As schools find themselves in this richness of diversity, they need to be attentive to what children bring as a framework, building upon their experiences, values, and background knowledge to introduce them to more public forms of literacy.

Dyson (1997) sees the issue to be one of identifying differences as problems or as possibilities. She describes this potential (to go either way) as an intersection of the many *horizontal* differences—that is, those differences of language, cultural style, familial circumstance, or other sociocultural and linguistic differences—with *vertical* differences—those where children fall on the very narrow band of abilities and skills that mark even young children as "smart" or "not," "ready" or "not," "at risk" or "not" via a kind of standardized achievement test (p. 11). She notes the teachers she worked with in this study of inner-city children "....worked hard to make visible children's competence and to acknowledge the breadth of language, symbolic and problem-posing and -solving skills needed in our world—without abandoning the need to straightforwardly help children learn traditional school knowledge and skills" (p. 12). Schools need to move away from equating horizontal differences with risk for children who are different from the dominant cultural group. Schools must create bridges to literacy for children of all backgrounds.

Key studies that provide ways to foster positive relationships among culture, language, and schooling include:

- Au and Mason's (1981, 1983) work with the Kamehameha School (KEEP) to construct a curriculum that was attentive to the native language structures of Hawaiian children shows the importance of a match between native language and dominant language as key to moving children into successful literacy experiences (cf. Gallimore, Boggs, & Jordan, 1974; Jordan, 1984, 1992).

- Delpit's (1986, 1988) work argues that many linguistic and ethnic minority students must be made aware of and taught the "language of power" (e.g., the conventions of written language and the academic register) to be successful in school.

- Goldenberg's (1987) ongoing work with Hispanic students in metropolitan Los Angeles as well as other diverse locations in California focuses on a view of cultural discontinuity rather than of cultural deprivation as a way to consider children's success in school. For example, many Hispanic families place more emphasis on moral development in preschool experiences whereas the school may expect the family to place a higher value on academic achievement. This difference in emphasis points out a discontinuity between cultures rather than confirming that some children lack particular experiences.

- Heath's (1983) study of three groups within an Appalachian town found the differences in language patterns and expectations affected school success. The school was not attentive to what some students did know (e.g., creative uses of oral language for storytelling).

- KEEP's work in collaboration with the Rough Rock Demonstration school (Jordan, 1995) showed that a "culturally responsive school"—that is, those schools that acknowledged the cultural heritage of students—provided a successful milieu for Native students. Teaching and learning in these schools acknowledged the differences in amount, initiation patterns, volume of talk, and the use of questions.

- Michael's (1981) study of "show and tell" showed how everyday language and the language of school often clashed—children were not able to make the transitions to school language without help from teachers aware of the discontinuity, and thus were at a disadvantage to progress according to school standards of language, especially the school value for linear, topic-centered, oral presentations.

- Philips' (1983) study of Native American students (Warm Springs Reservation in Oregon) found that differences between Native American students and a White teacher in language styles and expectations caused a lack of learning. School experiences that focused upon single performance, provided no opportunity for practice, and lacked support for learning in small groups did not match the cultural expectations for learning for Native American students.

- Street's (1995, pp.126-127) research on literacy practices and attitudes in middle-class homes revealed what he called a "relentless commitment to instruction in literacy." Children were engaged in literate activities expressly to teach them reading and writing. In many school settings, this explicit instruction in literacy is continued, but where teachers base the timing and amount of literacy instruction on the learner's needs, there can be a discontinuity between the home values for adult-determined literacy lessons and the school's use of learner-centered, learner-responsive literacy instruction to build on what the child already knows. The obverse can be equally true: Children from homes where literacy instruction wasn't provided come to school and are judged to be lacking, not ready to read.

- Taylor and Dorsey-Gaines' (1988) study of six inner-city families showed a great number and variety of early literacy experiences displayed within their everyday lives, but a mismatch between school expectations and the cultural expectations and interpretations. While there were many rich reading and writing experiences available to the children in their homes, school provided mainly workbook and drill-oriented experiences. This study points out the danger in global generalizations about the literacy needs of low socioeconomic status cultural and ethnic minority students.

- Wells' (1986) longitudinal study of preschool children in London found a critical relationship between the reading aloud to children and their success as readers at school. The amount of storybook reading children had experienced prior to beginning school was the single strongest factor in determining their later school success.

It is clear from a variety of indicators that there is a gap between the literacy achievement of minority students and those in the dominant cultural group. Educational anthropologists John Ogbu and Frederick Erickson offer two perspectives from which to consider the issues surrounding this disparity. Ogbu's (1981, 1990, 1993) work focuses on a theory of "cultural inversion": a phenomenon where minority students choose to fail to do well in school as a way to maintain their own culture rather than to become subsumed by the dominant culture. This suggests teachers must work to gain students' trust, so that students become willing to acquire the strategies and attitudes necessary for academic success. It is important to support positive connections between the home culture and school. For example, Erickson's (1993; Erickson & Mohatt, 1982) research describes the importance of "culturally responsive instruction" as a way of providing for success for minority students. He suggests teachers use communication patterns responsive to or compatible with the norms, beliefs, and values of students' home cultures.

In addition, parents of children not in the dominant cultural group must be supported to become partners with the school in their children's literacy development. It is not lack of interest in their children's school success that keeps these parents at a remove from the school. Rather it may be that the school lacks the appropriate strategies and mechanisms to involve them (Edwards, 1991, p. 210). Beyond giving generic advice to "read to your children," schools can share resources, demonstrate strategies, and otherwise invite parents into the literacy process.

Gay (1988) states that it is the variety of interests, aptitudes, motivations, experiences, and cultural conditioning that determine how, not whether, students can or cannot learn. For school, then, the learning context is very important, not simply how children achieve on a standardized test. How do we, as educators, begin to recognize when the mismatches occur? How do we know a child is not successful at reading because, for example, the texts don't match his experiences? There are many horizontal differences among children, but these are in themselves not positive or negative with regard to children's learning. It is when institutions (e.g., the school) equate or correlate these risk factors to academic deficiencies that they become problems rather than possibilities. The danger is a focus on narrow literacy skills, emphasizing or even distorting vertical differences. The issue is for the school to provide what the child needs now, not to explain away failure as the home's fault.

The underpinnings of oral language—the ways in which children have come to "mean" in their home culture—are critical to the development of written language modes of reading and writing. Reading is language. While the tasks of written language differ in many ways, the *processes* through which they are learned are, in principle, the same. However, the home language of students provides the foundation for the emergence of reading and writing behaviors. If there is a mismatch between the structures, values, and expectations of the home language and school language, children may be at a disadvantage for success in early reading tasks, and thus spend their entire school careers attempting to catch up.

Children at Risk of Failing to Succeed

> By making believe that failure is something kids do, as different from how it is something done to them, and then by explaining their failure in terms of other things they do, we likely contribute to the maintenance of school failure (McDermott, 1987, p. 363).

There are many characteristics associated with children who experience difficulty in learning to read. Individual differences are important, but should they lead to children's failure to succeed in school? While cultural factors are critical in consideration of these children, the complexity of our society and the structure of our schools encompass a much wider range of factors. Consideration of socioeconomic status, language minority (ESL/ bilingual), and other special needs are important. Invariably, these factors are often intertwined: For example, some remedial reading programs (most specifically Title I programs) are based upon the needs of children of poverty; often, this includes language minority children. The question remains, however: How can our schools best meet the needs of these children to support them in successful ways?

21

Allington (1977, 1980, 1983), Allington and McGill-Franzen (1989), Durkin (1978), and Hiebert (1983) describe the stark differences in teaching low-achieving students as compared to their more adept peers. Stanovich (1986) describes a "Matthew effect" in low-achieving readers: Capable readers get to read more books and engage in reinforcing activities such as talking and writing about what they've read while struggling readers get a steady diet of skill instruction and few opportunities to actually read real books. The evidence suggests that it is the amount of reading that differentiates low achieving students from high achieving students.

Allington and Walmsley (1995, p. 22) assert that throughout studies of effective instructional intervention with special student populations, no truly specialized materials or teaching strategies demonstrated advantages over the best teaching available in regular education classrooms (Larrivee, 1985; Lyons, 1989). What we see, rather, is that a particular instructional strategy used with at-risk children is not as important as simply attending to their needs (Allington & Walmsley, 1995, p. 253). This points to the need to provide equal access to school resources for all children to increase the chances of success for all in literacy learning (Kozol, 1991).

Poverty. As the number of children living in poverty increases, the impact of living without critical resources is increasingly apparent in the lack of school success of children in school. While many of these families possess a literacy that reflects their community and culture, they often do not have access to books and other print materials, either to borrow or to own; to varied childhood experiences such as trips to the zoo; to see everyday uses of literacy upon which school literacy activities are based (e.g., newspapers, shopping, entertainment); or to a wide variety of rich oral language interactions. While many of these children are of cultural and ethnic minority, many, too, are of European-American descent. Regardless of poor children's culture or ethnicity, there is a pattern of schools having low academic expectations for them. Teaching methods and instructional materials reflect this belief. Often, schools assume these children are capable only of low-level drill in basic skills. In addition, schools may provide such students with less qualified teachers, little opportunity to read real texts, and little access to interaction with more skilled readers. Moll (n.d., p. 62) states: "When 'disadvantaged' children are shown to succeed under modified instructional arrangements, it becomes clear that the problems these children face in school must be viewed, in great part, as a consequence of institutional arrangements that constrain children and teachers by not capitalizing fully on their talents, resources, and skills" (Diaz, Moll, & Mehan, 1986; Moll & S. Diaz, 1987).

When a commitment to modify instructional arrangements based upon current best practice is made, children of poverty gain opportunities to succeed (Allington, n.d.). For example:

- Purcell-Gates, McIntyre, and Dahl (1995) found that children from low socioeconomic backgrounds with little previous experience with print gained linguistic competence in story structure, vocabulary, and concepts about print when involved in experiences designed to promote this type of knowledge.

- Adams (1990) concluded that while it is true that some children can figure out the letter-sound system without much instruction, children with little exposure to reading and writing often need some explicit phonics instruction. Many rich experiences with reading and writing must support such instruction.

- Allington (1994a, 1994b) asserts that specifically because of the lack of experience and exposure, students considered at risk need more time to read—really read in real texts—in contrast to drills on particular skills.

- Snow and colleagues (1991) found a complex set of interactions of both home and school factors that influenced the successful literacy development of low-income children. The enormous impact of consistent, high-quality classroom instruction was clear; in situations where children did not have high levels of literacy support at home, anything less than high-quality instruction at school had dramatically negative impacts on school achievement (Allington & Cunningham, 1996).

- Edwards (1989, 1991) and others found that parent-directed book-reading interactions will allow at-risk children to acquire literacy skills that will help them become better readers at school. Some parents may need support in how to provide these experiences at home (Gallimore & Goldenberg, 1989; Mason, 1986; Teale, 1981, 1987).

English language acquisition. As immigration into the United States continues, many children enter school with a language other than English. These children have become fluent in this language via oral language processes parallel to those described earlier (Ellis, 1985; Hakuta, 1986). Snow (1992) suggests that a sociocultural perspective is most appropriate for defining literacy in light of language variety: Literacy can be defined in terms of what is appropriate to get along in one's culture for everyday life rather than solely upon an indefinable standard language. Thus, literacy is much more than simply being able to read and write; it is, rather, a set of complex tasks and behaviors that may, for some individuals, encompass the use of several languages and literacies. Ada (1980, p. 1) reminds us "no one learns to read twice": Learning to read in a first language, the language that encompasses those things familiar and meaningful, is critical to success in learning to read in a second language.

A recent study indicates that English-language learners receive lower grades, are judged by their teachers to have lower academic abilities, and score below their classmates on standardized tests of reading and math (Moss & Puma, 1995); statistics show that language minority students are 1.5 times more likely to drop out of school than native speakers (Cardenas, Robledo, & Waggoner, 1988). It is important to note that some (Carnegie Corporation, 1996) believe a constructive way in which to address the issue of second language learning is to promote learning two or more languages for all students.

Debate continues, however, on the best way to assist students as they learn English as their second language. Collier (1995) asserts it is a misassumption to believe that the first thing students must do is learn English, thus isolating the language from a broad complex of other issues. Much of the debate rests exactly here: Should students know English before they are allowed to join their peers in classrooms?

Cognitive and academic development in the first language has been found to have critically important and positive effects on second language learning (Bialystock, 1991; Collier, 1989, 1992; Garcia, 1994; Genesee, 1987, 1994; Thomas & Collier, 1997). Academic skills, literacy development, concept formation, subject knowledge, and strategy development learned in the first language will transfer to the second language. However, because literacy is socially situated, it is equally critical to provide a socioculturally supportive school environment that allows the first language and academic and cognitive development to flourish. Self-esteem and self-confidence are also critical components for success.

It is clear, however, in recent research syntheses within the field (August & Hakuta, 1997, p. 176; Cuevas, 1997) that native language use is advantageous in English language acquisition. This use is defined within a range from a firm commitment to a bilingual program to programs where although most instruction took place in English, native language was used to clarify and extend. The second language child makes sense of the second language by using many of the same strategies that worked so well in the acquiring the first language. What is different, however, is that the second language child already has an understanding of the meanings, uses, and purposes of language; he must now go on to learn how the second language—orally and in print—expresses those purposes, uses, and meanings (Lindfors, 1987, p. 445). Oral language learning is a lifelong process (Berko Gleason, 1993; Collier, 1992); school age children are still acquiring subtle knowledge in oral language expertise.

Krashen's (1981, 1982; Krashen & Terrell, 1983) work has had important impact on second language learning and teaching. His theories are based in current beliefs about first language oral acquisition. Basic principles include (1983, pp. 20-21): Understanding precedes speaking; production is allowed to emerge in stages; the goals of instruction are communicative in nature; and activities must "lower the affective filter of students," that is, provide interesting and relevant topics and tasks and encourage the expression of ideas, thoughts, opinions, and feelings.

It is important to understand the consequences of various program designs for students learning English:

- In U.S. schools where all instruction is given through the second language (i.e., English), non-native speakers with no schooling in their first language take seven to ten years to reach age- and grade-level norms (Cummins, 1981; Thomas & Collier, 1997).

- Immigrant students who have had two to three years of schooling in a first language in their home countries take at least five to seven years to reach age and grade level norms (Cummins, 1981; Thomas & Collier, 1997).

- Non-native speakers schooled in a second language for part or all of the day typically do reasonably well in early years; however, from fourth grade, when academic and cognitive demands of the curriculum increase rapidly, students with little or no academic and cognitive development in their first language fail to maintain positive gains (Collier, 1995; Thomas & Collier, 1997).

- Students who have spent four to seven years in a quality bilingual program sustain academic achievement and outperform monolingually schooled students in the upper grades (Thomas & Collier, 1997).

It is clear that learning to read in the first language supports success with reading in the second language (cf. August & Hakuta, 1997; Cuevas, 1997; Roberts, 1994):

- Oral and written language are reciprocal: that is, many experiences in oral language—conversations, reading aloud, and so on—in both languages are critical.

- Environments filled with print examples in both languages are important to successful acquisition (Hudelson, 1987). For example, children's literature in both languages should be in classroom and school libraries for children to access at both school and home; newspapers and other examples of community literacy should be available in both languages at home and at school; signage in classrooms should be in both languages as appropriate.

- A variety of authentic opportunities to read and write in both languages should be available in the classroom (Janopoulous, 1986; Moll, 1992).

- Literacy skills related to decoding tasks of reading do indeed transfer between languages (Bialystock, 1997; Goodman, Goodman, & Flores, 1979; Hudelson, 1987; Mace-Matluck, 1982). However, these must be contextualized within meaningful, authentic tasks and texts for full transfer to occur.

- English vocabulary is a primary determinant of reading comprehension for second language readers. Those whose first language has many cognates with English do have an advantage in English vocabulary recognition, but often require explicit instruction to optimize transfer for comprehension (Garcia & Nagy, 1993, as cited in August & Hakuta, 1997).

- Self-confidence is supported as children learn to read in their first language, then are allowed to transfer this knowledge to reading in a second language. Ada (1980) asserts children taught in this way will "have better opportunities for discovering the meaning and joy of reading" (p. 2).

Many studies support the notion of a balanced literacy program as appropriate for students whose first language is not English, that is, programs that provide a balance of explicit instruction and student-directed activities that incorporate aspects of both traditional and meaning-based curricula (Goldenberg & Gallimore, 1991; Goldenberg & Sullivan, 1994; Moll, 1988). However, no one right way to educate English language learners can be determined; different approaches are necessary because of the great diversity of conditions faced by schools and the varying experiences of English learners with literacy and schooling in their first language (August & Hakuta, 1997, p. 174). Moll (1988) observes that effective teachers share a belief in the power of their teaching, but create their own instructional programs that are attuned to the needs of their students. Clearly, educators must rethink their assumptions about the literacy skills of students new to English in their first language as well as in English. They may find a potential for reciprocity between the two languages.

Special needs. The programs for students with special needs encompass varied definitions in regard to individual students. For some students, an Individual Education Program (IEP) might result in participation in a Title I program (determined by a gap between achievement and grade level); for others, needs may dictate a Special Education program which is warranted when there are handicapping conditions, the most common being Learning Disabled (LD) or Reading Disabled (RD). Spear-Swerling & Sternberg (1996) contend "...there is currently little educational basis for differentiating school-labeled children with Reading Disability (RD) from other kinds of poor readers" (p. 4). And yet, public perceptions (often fed by the media) are describing a large portion of the school population as learning disabled because they are struggling readers.

Educational definitions of reading disability contain the three elements that historically have been central to definitions of the concept: the notion that children with RD are achieving well below their true potential for learning; the assumption that RD is due to an intrinsic deficit (sometimes described in psychological terms as a "disorder in processing" but assumed to have a biological cause); and exclusionary criteria, which rule out other disorders (e.g., mental retardation, emotional disturbance, or sensory impairment) and the environment as the primary causes of RD (Spear-Swerling & Sternberg, 1996). Many find research in the RD field is especially contradictory and confusing. There are isolated research findings to support almost any position one wishes to take. Research has shown (Haynes & Jenkins, 1986; Vanecko, Ames, & Archambault, 1980) mildly handicapped special education students received significantly less reading instruction than remedial students, and there is evidence that both groups actually received less reading instruction than better readers (Allington & Walmsley, 1995, pp. 20-21).

There is debate as to whether struggling readers—of any definition, but particularly those determined to have disabilities—need qualitatively different instruction. Some argue that these students need frequent, intensive, explicit, and individual support and direction from teachers (Rhodes & Dudley-Marling, 1996, p. 29), but within authentic and meaningful experiences that are not unlike those offered to other students in the classroom. Others argue for specific types of instruction that focus upon the specific needs of such readers as different from other students in the classroom, usually within the range of phonological skills that are taught as contextualized in meaningful texts (Spear-Swerling & Sternberg, 1996). Still others believe that a sole focus on decoding—learning specific phonemic awareness and phonic knowledge tasks—is the appropriate type of instruction, before the addition of reading in meaningful texts (Carnine & Grossen, 1993; Grossen & Carnine, 1990; Juel, 1994).

What does the research show in regard to instructional practices? Spear-Swerling and Sternberg (1996) observe that current research in reading instruction is only slowly making an impact within special education/remedial programs. Instruction within these programs still often focuses solely upon isolated drill. While many children in such programs do need some type of explicit instruction, like any child learning to read they also require many other types of instruction to succeed. These include instruction in strategy use, practicing in appropriate texts, and employing metacognitive strategies.

Implications for struggling readers. It appears that context is critical to dealing with the variety of needs of struggling readers. While there is no one method that can be found, nor is there any one definition of a struggling reader, teachers must be aware of the child's background (social, economic, cultural) and needs (type of variability, learning style).

These factors are critical to providing supportive environments for struggling readers:

- *Access and opportunity to a wide variety of reading materials.* These materials need to reflect meaning and authenticity for individual readers as well as a manageable level of text.

- *Motivating readers to want to read and to want to engage in reading.* Readers need to see reasons and purposes for reading that relate to their perception of the world.

- *Providing time to really read in real texts.* Struggling readers need more time to read, and need more time with high-quality instruction (Allington & Cunningham, 1996).

- *Supportive instruction in the "how-tos" of reading.* Teachers, peers, parents, and other sophisticated users offer demonstrations, guidance, and feedback in how to read.

- *Self-esteem and confidence, which play integral roles in successful reading development.* Children need to feel positive about their attempts and their progress.

- *High expectation for success in a supported environment.*

Experiences and programs designed for children who struggle with learning to read reflect these factors. For example, Reading Recovery (Clay, 1972; Deford, Lyons, & Pinnell, 1991) is a program which focuses on short-term (usually less than one year), intensive, one-to-one intervention with children who struggle very early on (usually in first grade) and which occurs in addition to regular classroom experiences. Roller (1996) suggests a workshop model where children choose from a wide variety of reading materials, participate in literature discussion groups and carry out personal writing projects in the classroom paired with one-to-one and small-group instruction during other times of the day. While the organizational structures may differ, these designs continue to focus upon rich, meaningful language experiences as the context for a variety of types of instruction.

Variability (e.g., in literacy experiences, preferences, understandings, abilities, and language) must be acknowledged as a central part of understanding students and their needs (Roller, 1996, p. 9). Alternative ways of viewing individual differences provide insight into a variety of organizational patterns for instruction that can best meet the needs of all children. In the following section, these factors and important understandings are discussed in detail in relationship to how all children learn to read.

Learning to Read: Core Understandings

Reading as Language

1. Reading is a construction of meaning from text. It is an active, cognitive, and affective process.

Readers do not take in print and receive words off the page. They actively engage with the text and build their own understanding. This is a social process: That is, it occurs within a situation whose participants, time, place, and expectation will impact the reader (Halliday, 1973, 1975). As with all modes of language (reading and writing, listening and speaking), the ultimate purpose of the reader is to construct meaning by interacting with the text (Pearson, Roehler, Dole, & Duffy, 1990; Rosenblatt, 1938/1976, 1978).

To support this construction of meaning, instruction should include explicitly taught comprehension strategies for reading narrative as well as expository text. Many and varied opportunities should be provided to require the reader to use and practice strategies that aid the reader in prereading, during reading, and postreading comprehension.

2. Background knowledge and prior experience are critical to the reading process.

The work of Anderson and Pearson (1984) and Rumelhart (1980) has demonstrated the importance of prior knowledge in reading. According to this view, called schema theory, readers understand what they read only as it relates to what they already know. Because text is not fully explicit, readers must draw from their existing knowledge in order to understand it. Sweet's (1993, p. 3) summary suggests prior knowledge should be looked at in two ways:

- Overall prior knowledge: that which represents the sum of knowledge individuals have acquired as a result of their cumulative experiences both in and out of school.

- Specific prior knowledge: that which represents the particular information an individual needs in order to understand text that deals with a certain topic. This can be of two types:

  - text-specific knowledge that calls for understanding about the type of text

  - topic-specific knowledge that calls for understanding something about the topic

It is important for teachers to come to understand the range of background knowledge students bring to school—both overall and specific. Opportunities to expand overall background knowledge are provided in classrooms via a wide variety of experiences and discussions to provide a wide knowledge of the world from which to interact, including teacher read-alouds, student independent reading times, written response to what has been read, and access to many books and other reading materials. The more students read and write, the more their prior knowledge grows, which in turn strengthens their ability to construct meaning as they read (Allington & Cunningham, 1996; Sweet, 1993).

Once students understand the functions of print, they can better learn the forms. Activating only students' topical prior knowledge without helping them to consider the actual structure of the text does not improve their meaning-making abilities (Beck, Omanson, & McKeown, 1982). Moustafa (1997) describes the need to learn the "language of print"; Clay (1972) stresses the importance of learning "the concepts of print." This is also the case for students learning English as a second language: Using their background knowledge of how they use their first language (in all language modes, speaking and listening, reading and writing) offers the scaffold necessary to learn the second language (Roberts, 1994).

The knowledge of how print works is essential and must operate in tandem with a reader's topical knowledge to construct meaning from text. Teachers can effectively improve these abilities when they activate all levels of students' prior knowledge appropriately.

3. Social interaction is essential in learning to read.

Children need the opportunity to interact with both peers and adults in a wide variety of settings as they are learning and practicing language and literacy knowledge, skills, and strategies. It is important to talk about what is read as well as what one does as a reader. Vygotsky (1978) emphasizes the importance of social interactions to actually drive any learning process. Bruner (1975) and Applebee and Langer (1983) elaborate upon this notion with their descriptions of "scaffolding"—the interaction between the learner and more sophisticated others that provides guidance, support, and models as new things are learned. In this process, metacognition develops. This is the ability to be aware of what one does as a reader as well as to talk about what is read, and to consciously realize problems and reach solutions for them (Baker & Brown, 1984; cf. Sweet, 1993). Children need the opportunity to interact with both peers and adults in a wide variety of settings as they are learning and practicing language and literacy knowledge, skills, and strategies.

Critical knowledge of both the reading processes and what one does as a strategic reader is built through discussion (Eeds & Wells, 1989; Langer, 1991). Goldenberg (1993) suggests an instructional conversation model that combines conversational aspects (the supportive elements of the discussion) and instructional aspects (the lesson focus). The teacher takes the role of a mentor, urging children to think about how they are thinking rather than only what they are thinking. Listening carefully to how children construct their responses provides an opportunity to discuss their use and knowledge of strategies with them. Teachers phase in to demonstrate and name particular strategies, then phase out to give students a chance to use the new strategies on their own (Walker, 1996). This model provides the support of scaffolding and modeling, then allows children to practice and implement new knowledge about reading on their own. In this way, understanding of the reading process and metacognitive strategy develop through social interaction.

4. Reading and writing develop together.

Both reading and writing are constructive processes (Pearson & Tierney, 1984; Squire, 1983). A similar, if not the same, level of intellectual activity underlies both reading and writing: Interactions between the reader/writer and text lead to new knowledge and interpretations of text (Langer, 1986; Clay, 1977; cf. Sweet, 1993).

Research shows that writing leads to improved reading achievement, reading leads to better writing performance, and combined instruction leads to improvements in both areas (Tierney & Shanahan, 1991). It has also been found that engaging learners in many combined reading and writing experiences leads to a higher level of thinking than when either process is taught alone. Since thinking is a critical part of meaning construction, students will become better thinkers if they are taught in classrooms where meaning is actively constructed through reading and writing (cf. Sweet, 1993).

When children have opportunities to write their own stories, to read their own and others' stories, and to write in response to reading, they are able to employ much of their knowledge of reading in meaningful and purposeful ways. Wilde (1992) and others (e.g., Clarke, 1988) have found the use of invented spelling as young children write provides a window into how their understanding of the alphabetic principle of language is evolving while they are learning important phonic knowledge.

Reading as Learning

5. Reading involves complex thinking.

Research across disciplines, but particularly in cognitive and developmental psychology and education, shows that reading (and all language modes) is the result of particular cognitive processes (Association for Supervision and Curriculum Development [ASCD], 1997; Caine & Caine, 1991, 1997). Readers consciously orchestrate a variety of thinking skills to make meaning of the texts they read. They rely upon a wide range of background knowledge, both about the world they live in and the ways in which they can get meaning from a text. They know they must make many types of decisions and choices in order to do this all effectively. (Also refer to Reading as Language in this document, Nos. 1 and 2.)

While there are many theories and models pertaining to the workings of written language, most are in agreement that written language relies upon four cueing systems, representing types of knowledge the reader uses as he interacts with text: (a) pragmatic (social context); (b) semantic (meaning); (c) syntactic (structural); and (d) grapho-phonic (the alphabetic, orthographic, sound-symbol aspects). All of these must be operating in tandem for optimal meaning. Effective readers are active in the reading process as decision makers and problem solvers, and as they demonstrate independent thinking (cf. Ruddell, Ruddell, & Singer, 1994).

For example, as students read a piece of literature they respond to it by using their prior knowledge to construct meaning. This transaction with the text results in the construction of their own personal meaning (Rosenblatt, 1938/1976, 1978). Response and discussion helps students develop metacognitive skills important to constructing meaning (Palincsar & Brown, 1984). In this way, their reading can move from response to analysis (cf. Sweet, 1993).

Current educational reform highlights the need for critical thinking and problem solving. Models of the reading process that portray reading as thinking support this perspective. The emphasis has come to rest upon the need for higher standards and expectations for students within public schools, represented in both National Standards (International Reading Association/National Council of Teachers of English, 1996) and state standards such as the

Washington state Essential Academic Learning Requirements (EALRS) (Commission on Student Learning, 1996).

6. Environments rich in literacy experiences, resources, and models facilitate reading development.

Children need many opportunities to interact with print in meaningful ways. Both social and physical factors are important for creating a supportive environment for successful literacy acquisition and development. Teale (1982) views the development of early literacy as the result of children's involvement in reading and writing activities mediated by more literate others. While the physical context is important, it is the social interactions of these activities that gives them so much significance in the child's development. These interactions—with others and within a variety of print settings—teach children the societal functions and conventions of reading and writing and help them link reading with enjoyment and satisfaction, thus increasing their desire to engage in meaningful literacy activities.

Physical environment. Historically, educators and theorists have emphasized the importance of physical environment in learning and literacy development. Pestalozzi (cited in Rusk & Scotland, 1979), Piaget (Piaget & Inhelder, 1969) and Froebel (1974) described real-life environments in which learning flourished among young children, recognizing the use of appropriate manipulative materials could foster literacy development. Vygotsky (1978) supports the notion that learning takes place as the child interacts with peers and adults in social settings and conducive environments. Children in purposefully arranged rooms demonstrate more creative productivity, greater use of language-related activities, more engaged and exploratory behavior, and more social interaction and cooperation than did children in randomly or poorly defined settings (Moore, 1986). Factors critical to an effective physical environment include:

- Physical setting has an active and pervasive influence on the both the teacher's and the students' activities and attributes (Loughlin & Martin, 1987; Morrow, 1990; Rivlin & Weinstein, 1984). For example, the inclusion of writing centers, library corners complete with a wide variety of materials to read (e.g., genres and levels of difficulty), areas to read independently and with others, and opportunities to use literacy in play are important.

- Rooms partitioned into smaller spaces facilitate peer and verbal interaction and imaginative, associative and cooperative play more effectively than do rooms with large open spaces (Field, 1980).

- A wide variety of print materials, including classroom and school library collections and community resources, e.g., public libraries, increases access to literacy experiences (Allington & Cunningham, 1996; Krashen, 1995).

Storybook reading. Rich and supportive literacy environments include opportunities to be read to by parents, caregivers, and others; observe adults who read often themselves; receive adult support for children's literacy activities; and experience routine use of materials for reading and writing at home and at school (Durkin, 1974-75; Taylor, 1983; Teale, 1984). Ideal settings are oriented to real-life situations; materials are chosen to give children the chance to explore and experiment (Morrow, 1996; Laughlin & Martin, 1987). In schools, program and environment must be coordinated to support the activities and needs of students (Spivak, 1973).

Storybook reading has been shown to have one of the greatest impacts on a child's access to a "literate environment." It provides both the social interaction and physical inclusion and demonstrations of print material. For example:

- Introducing and using literature with young children correlates positively with development of sophisticated language structures, including vocabulary and syntax (Chomsky, 1972).

- Children are engaging in their most intellectually demanding work when they share ideas and opinions about stories, and share experiences related to stories read or told to them (Dyson, 1987; Sweet, 1993).

- As children hear stories told and read, they learn the structure as well as the linguistic features of stories or narrative text (Cox & Sulzby, 1984). Children often display this knowledge by "talking like a book" when they pretend to read their favorite stories (Pappas & Brown, 1987).

- Storybook reading is most effective for developing children's ability to understand stories when it involves far more than reading aloud the words of an author. It is as much the verbal interaction between adult and child during the read-aloud experience as the read-aloud event itself that provides for a positive learning experience for the child (Teale & Sulzby, 1987; Morrow, 1988; Morrow, O'Connor, & Smith, 1990). Readers construct meaning as they interact with peers and adults in discussing stories (Jett-Simpson, 1989). Whether the reading aloud occurs between a parent and child or a teacher and a classroom of children, using interactive strategies such as story-based discussions along with storybook reading helps children construct meaning and understand stories that are read to them (cf. Sweet, 1993).

Language development has been found to correlate with reading success, and both can be improved by regular use of children's literature in read-aloud situations both at home and at school (Cullinan,1987). Bisset (1969) found that children in classrooms that included their own collections of literature read and looked at books 50 percent more often than did children whose classrooms housed no such collections. It is clear, then, that it is important to provide children daily with positive experiences involving stories and other literature that include reading and telling stories; dealing with stories through literal, interpretive, and critical discussions; integrating literature into themes being studied throughout the curriculum; and encouraging children to share books they have read, to respond to literature through written and oral language, and to participate regularly in social periods set aside for reading and writing (Hoffman, Roser, & Farest, 1988; Morrow, 1996; Morrow, O'Connor, & Smith, 1990).

Classroom communities. While social interaction, particularly at home, has been described as a critical component of language/literacy acquisition earlier in this document, it is important to highlight its importance within the learning environments of young learners at school as well. For example, in school situations cooperative and collaborative work which includes social interaction in small groups has been shown to increase both achievement and productivity (Johnson & Johnson, 1987; Slavin, 1983). Cazden (1986) also notes that peer interaction allows students to attempt a range of roles usually unavailable to them by traditional student-teacher structures.

Classrooms can be viewed as a community, much as the everyday communities students come from. There are appropriate social structures and expectations for those social structures; often, these evolve from the interactions among the teacher and the students in the classroom as well as from the expectations of "doing school" (Bloome, 1991). Effective classrooms for teaching and learning language and literacy build and respect community (Pearson, 1996). That is, they have respect for the backgrounds and knowledge each student contributes to the community, using this as a foundation from which to build a "literate" classroom community that fosters an understanding for the purposeful use of literacy in everyday lives. These social constructs are critical to successful literacy learning. It is important for teachers to come to understand the language and social structures of the cultures of their students, and to respect their role in tandem with the learning typical to "doing school."

7. Engagement in the reading task is key in successfully learning to read.

Children must be motivated to want to read for authentic purposes, connected to their own lives in meaningful ways. Cambourne (1988) describes four essential elements of engagement: (a) Learners must be seen as potential doers both personally and by those around them; (b) learners must see learning as personally meaningful; (c)learning must be perceived as low risk by the learner; and (d) learners must have the opportunity to bond with other doers.

Motivation is essential to engagement during a literacy event. A motivated individual initiates and continues a particular activity, returning to a task with sustained engagement, even as it becomes difficult (Maehr, 1976). Factors that lead to motivation and engagement include:

- Challenge, choice, and collaboration tend to motivate children to read. Researchers have found that experiences which afford students the opportunity for success, challenge, choice, and social collaborations are likely to promote motivation (Gambrell, Palmer, & Coding, 1993, Gambrell, Almasi, Xie, & Heland, 1995; Morrow, 1996).

- The learning environment must enable a student to perceive the challenge in the activity as one that he or she can accomplish. When the task is completed, the student must perceive success (Ford, 1992; McCombs, 1989; Spaulding, 1992).

- Self-selection of tasks instills intrinsic motivation (Morrow, 1992).

- Collaboration with a teacher or with peers in learning tasks finds children intrinsically motivated and likely to get more done than if they work alone (Brandt, 1990; Oldfather, 1993).

To be engaged readers, students must recognize the value of reading and their own potential as readers and learners. There is growing consensus that engagement with reading and with learning more generally is likely to lead to greater success in school (Morrow & Weinstein, 1986; National Academy of Education, 1991; Wang, Haertel, & Walberg, 1990). Literacies found at home and within the community foster desire and purpose to read; they are a means by which one becomes a member of a community of readers and society at large. Schools must build upon this background knowledge of literacy. Reading instruction should include diverse texts and diverse opportunities to interact with texts, rather than be limited to certain materials and procedures.

Research on reading engagement from the reader's perspective has found that high school students who are not effective readers lack the critical component of engagement (Greenleaf, 1997). This work has found such students:

- Do not appear to be motivated to read when they have no personal connection to the text

- Seem to be disengaged from reading, affectively and cognitively; reading is seen as an entirely school-based activity with no impact on their present or future lives outside of school

- Are not fluent or frequent readers; are limited by their prior lack of access to literate discourse

The role of engagement is becoming clear: If children are not engaged in reading, their ability to read will not develop. In general, the centrality of engagement appears in the following principles (Guthrie, 1997, p. 3):

- Children learn to be literate through engagement.

- Engaged learners want to understand.

- Children possesses intrinsic motivations for interacting with text.

- Readers use cognitive skills to understand and share knowledge by talking with teachers and peers.

- Engagements are valuable in themselves, but they also lead to achievement

- Unfortunately, some students disengage: If students struggle with learning to read and write, they lose the desire to read.

- If reading is not personally meaningful, children lose their interest and a decrease in achievement ensues.

A classroom providing opportunities for all children to engage in reading might include (Guthrie, 1997, p. 3):

- Reading lessons designed to develop long-term motivation, knowledge, and social competence as well as reading skill

- Effective lessons designed as frequently by students as by teachers

- Different sets of time and organization

- Outcomes designed for the long term; use of portfolios and performance-based assessments

- Lots of talk—students are involved and social

- Skill instruction embedded in meaningful engagements

8. Children's understandings of print are not the same as adults' understandings.

Learning strategies for children, as well as their conceptualizations of the world, differ much from those of adults. Y. Goodman (cited in Teale & Sulzby, 1986) offers this summation:

> In general, it is now understood that children do not view the world or the concepts within the world in the same way as adults do...when children are reading and writing they are making sense out of or through print. Eventually readers and writers of English intuitively come to know that written language in English is based upon certain alphabetic principles. However, this knowledge is not a prerequisite for children's learning to read and write. Children perceive written language and provide evidence that they are aware that there is a message in that transaction when they read "brake the car" in response to a stop sign or "toothpaste" in response to a Crest toothpaste label.... (p. 5).

Children's understanding of print differs from that of adults. The crucial question is what understandings are vital (e.g., that print carries a message and it should make sense) at the earliest stages of reading, and what more sophisticated conventional understandings children grow into as they learn to read independently.

For example, many young learners are not good at learning analytically, abstractly, or auditorily (Carbo, 1987). Therefore, for most young children, it is harder to learn aspects of language and literacy through their parts without some understanding of the whole of language, that is, with a concept of the meanings words and sentences convey. How young children begin to develop phonemic awareness and phonic knowledge provides important insight into how children perceive language in ways different from adults.

The aspects of linguistic and metalinguistic awareness—children's "knowledge of wordness" (cf. Clay, 1979; Yaden & Templeton, 1986)—must be included in this discussion. Children must become aware of language as written, then gain more sophisticated concepts about print, including being able to talk about and describe its aspects and processes as they understand them. They will need to know about the parts as well as the whole, and that it all makes meaningful sense. This is important to make explicit, as children who fail to see the very nature and purposes of reading are often those who are seen to be at risk of not learning to read successfully.

How do children begin to perceive the individual sounds of language? Research has shown that children might not see this task in the same way that adults do:

- Bruce (1964) demonstrated that young children have difficulty manipulating phonemes. Others (Rosner, 1974; Liberman, Shankweiler, Fischer, & Carter, 1974; Ehri & Wilce, 1980; Mann, 1986; Treiman & Baron, 1981; Tumner & Nesdale, 1985) looked at phoneme manipulation from a variety of perspectives, all with similar results. This research shows that young children don't analyze speech into phonemes before they begin to read in the way literate adults have traditionally thought they do. It appears that it is much easier for young children to first identify spoken syllables than to abstract either words or sounds from the stream of speech (see Adams, 1990, p. 296-300; Moustafa, 1997).

- Berdiansky, Cronnell, and Koehler (1969), building upon the work of Venezky (1967), found that the complexity of the relationship to sounds in words was in the combination of the letters that produced unique sets of sounds. None of the letter sounds are all that "regular" within the contexts of words because of the interrelationships within the structure of each word. There is not a small, manageable number of rules as some suggest. Rather, letter sound correspondences are represented by a complex web of relationships (Hanna, et al., 1966; Moustafa, 1997; Venezky, 1970).

- The ability to segment phonemes appears to be a consequence of literacy development, or is at least in tandem with it (Lie, 1991; Mann, 1986; Morias, Bertelson, Cary, & Alegria, 1986; Perfetti, Beck, Bell, & Hughes, 1987; Read, Yun-Fei, Hong-Yin, & Bao-Gin, 1986; Winner, Landerl, Linortner, & Hummer, 1991).

So, what do children do as they are learning to read in this complex system of sounds and symbols? From observations of oral language development, we know that young children are capable of using a variety of quite sophisticated strategies. They do much the same as they learn written language:

- Young children become sensitive to rhyme at an early age (Goswami & Bryant, 1990).

- Young children do not initially hear individual phonemes; rather they hear the initial phoneme, and the spoken syllable. *Onsets* are any consonants before a vowel in a spoken syllable and *rimes* are the vowel and any consonants after it (Adams, 1990, pp. 308-328; Moustafa, 1997; Treiman, 1986; Treiman & Chafetz, 1987; Treiman & Baron, 1981; Wylie & Durrell, 1970).

- Young children are competent at analyzing spoken words into onsets and rimes but not into phonemes when onsets or rimes consist of more than one phoneme (Calfee, 1977; Goswami & Bryant, 1990; Liberman, et al., 1974; Treiman, 1983, 1985).

- Young children develop an awareness of syllables early and can do so without instruction (Wimmer, Landerl, Linortner, & Hummer, 1991; Morias, Bertelson, Cary, & Algeria, 1986).

- Young children who are beginning to read make analogies between familiar and unfamiliar print words to pronounce unfamiliar print words. Children make these analogies at the onset-rime level rather than at the phonemic level (Goswami, 1986, 1988).

When designing instructional experiences, teachers must consider those things that support children's learning about print that are appropriate to their current understandings.

9. **Children develop phonemic awareness and knowledge of phonics through a variety of literacy opportunities, models, and demonstrations.**

Much time and effort has been invested in investigations and consequent discussions about how children learn to apply the alphabetic principle—those understandings of print that are the critical difference between oral and written language—in order to read and write. The importance of the development of early word identification skill is evident (Carnine & Grossen, 1993; Juel, 1991; Pearson, 1993; Stanovich, 1991). Unfortunately, these discussions have become as much political as educational. Currently, the debate has come to focus primarily upon two factors: (a) the place of phonemic awareness (discerning that spoken language is composed of separate speech sounds; the ability to segment the speech stream of a spoken word) and (b) phonics (the teaching of particular parts of language, specifically rules for phoneme-grapheme relationships) in early reading instruction. Many studies point to phonemic awareness as a predictor of early reading success; however, it is also clear that it is but one factor important to the development of effective reading strategies to read for meaning. Also, there is agreement that at least a basic knowledge of letter-sound relationships (phonics) is a necessary, but not sufficient, strategy used by successful readers. The question is thus how much, how, when and under what circumstances phonemic awareness and phonic knowledge are included in instruction. It is important for all stakeholders to stand back and consider: Are we asking the right questions in regard to what children need to know, based upon what we now know?

The current intensity of this debate has led the International Reading Association, long known for maintaining that no single approach to reading instruction can be dictated as being best for every student, to issue a position statement (1997b) asserting three basic principles regarding phonics and the teaching of reading:

1. **The teaching of phonics is an important aspect of beginning reading instruction.** This only suggests there is nearly unanimous regard for its importance, not unanimity in agreement as to methodology.

2. **Classroom teachers in the primary grades do value and do teach phonics as part of their reading program.** Effective teachers make appropriate instructional decisions for the inclusion of phonics based upon their knowledge of children and their language development. The document concludes that "...programs that constrain teachers from using their professional judgment in making instructional decisions about what is best in phonics instruction for students simply get in the way of good teaching practices" (IRA, 1997b, n.p.).

3. **Phonics instruction, to be effective in promoting independence in reading, must be embedded in the context of a total reading/language arts program.** Specific

instruction in phonics takes on meaning for the learner when it is within meaningful contexts of language use (e.g., interesting and informative books, nursery rhymes, poetry, and songs) that provide patterns and structures to support their understanding (IRA, 1997b).

Perspectives at the heart of the debate. In light of the passionate debates that have arisen, it is even more critical for teachers to understand broadly and deeply the aspects of the alphabetic principle as it pertains to the teaching and learning of reading. It is also important to understand that there is more than one perspective from which to view reading; most commonly, reading is seen as either a process of decoding or as a process of constructing meaning (see pp. 7-9 in this document). Furthermore, knowledge of the reading process continues to emerge, often leading to more questions to pursue in order to better understand the processes of becoming literate. As Weaver, Gillmeister-Krause, and Vento-Zogby (1996, n.p.) note:

> ...[those who believe reading is a construction of meaning] point out that too much attention to phonics can detract from the construction of meaning, while [those who believe reading is decoding] cite correlations between tests of phonemic awareness and scores on standardized tests as evidence that phonemic awareness and phonics must be taught early to promote reading achievement—that is, high standardized test scores. Another major difference: Researchers who have studied emergent literacy (e.g., Harste, et al., 1984) point out that phonics knowledge is gained in the process of becoming a reader and writer, while those who have examined correlations between phonemic awareness and reading test scores note that phonemic awareness is a requisite to becoming an *independent* reader (e.g., Beck & Juel, 1995). Note, however, that the two ideas are compatible: Independent readers may have developed phonemic awareness in the process of becoming readers and writers, and in fact there is substantial evidence that this happens (Moustafa, 1995; Mann, 1986; Morias, Bertelson, Cary, & Alegria, 1986; Winner, Landerl, Linortner, & Hummer, 1991).

A caveat in understanding correlational research must be made: Correlation simply means that the two things are observed to occur together; it says nothing about whether one causes the other—for example, whether phonemic awareness leads to independent reading, whether learning to read results in phonemic awareness, or whether they interact and support each other's development (Weaver, Gillmeister-Krause, & Vento-Zogby, 1996; Moustafa, 1997). Correlation is not causation; thus, interpretations of research data must be careful in their generalizations.

Research in linguistics, cognitive and developmental psychology, anthropology, sociology, and education have shown that when dealing with print, several levels of information are available to assist the reader to make sense of the text. These include grapho-phonic, semantic, syntactic, and pragmatic (see pp. 7-9, 30 of this document). In this way, reading is much more complex than consideration of only the "visible" or print levels (Moustafa, 1997). At least, it appears that phonemic awareness and phonic knowledge develop simultaneously as children have many varied experiences with print, supported and guided by a knowledgeable other.

Several key studies have been used to frame the debate over phonics. These fall into two general categories: those that assert the primacy of phonics instruction in learning to read, and those that show phonics instruction as but one of many factors in learning to read.

Those that highlight the primacy of phonics instruction include:

- Jeanne Chall's (1967/1983) work suggests that systematic phonics instruction is a valuable component of beginning reading instruction within the complementary context of connected and meaningful reading (cf. Adams, 1990). Others point out, though, that Chall's findings of a positive correlation between systematic phonics and higher scores on tests of reading and spelling "achievement" only holds through the primary grades; beyond grade 4, the correlation ceases (Purcell-Gates, McIntrye, & Freppon, 1995; Shannon, 1996).

- Adams' (1990) recent review of research concludes that phonemic awareness and phonic knowledge instruction is a critical factor for success in early reading. While her work is praised by many for its thoroughness, many who view reading as a construction of meaning find this perspective to be missing particularly in regard to the sociocultural contexts of literacy.

- Foorman and her colleagues (1995, and forthcoming with Francis, Beeler, & Fletcher) have continued to conduct studies that look at how children with training in phonemic awareness and phonics knowledge fare, most recently in comparison to children participating in a "whole language" curriculum. While the most recent study is not yet published, preliminary findings show a positive impact on decoding of training in phonemic awareness. However, the children in the "whole language" classrooms tended to fare better on comprehension tests.

Those that highlight phonics instruction as one factor in learning to read include:

- Cooperative Research Program in Primary Reading Instruction (First Grade Studies) (Bond & Dykstra, 1967). Bond and Dykstra concluded that no one approach is so much better in all situations that it should be considered a best method. Even more generally, and probably more importantly for instructional considerations, they found that no matter what the program, the quality of teaching made the difference in the instruction. The implication is that to improve reading instruction, both programs and classroom delivery must be improved (Adams, 1990).

- Follow Through Studies (Stebbins, St. Pierre, Proper, Anderson, & Cerva, 1977). While the study focused upon a wide variety of models, no one model proved to be more effective than others on conceptual measures. Advocates of strong systematic phonics instruction continue to find data in regard to one of the sites using the Distar program—a highly structured and highly focused systematic teaching of the alphabet—as consistently showing the best reading achievement within the data. However, there continues to be much debate over the validity of these results (House, Glass, McLean, & Walker, 1978).

- *Becoming a Nation of Readers* (Anderson, Heibert, Scott, & Wilkinson, 1985). The authors state: "Phonics instruction should aim to teach only the most important and regular of letter-to-sound relationships....once the basic relationships have been taught, the best way to get children to refine and extend their knowledge of letter-sound correspondences is through repeated opportunities to read. If this position is correct, then much phonics instruction is overly subtle and probably unproductive" (p. 38).

- High/Scope Studies (Schweinhart, Weikart, & Larner, 1986). This research looked at three programs for emergent readers, Distar, whole language, and traditional. Whole language appeared to give children important first knowledge about reading while the most structured of the programs, Distar, appeared to severely limit the long-term social potential of its participants. While this study showed diverse curriculum models can be equally effective, it also showed the vital importance of social interaction in successful teaching and learning.

It is important to acknowledge the important contribution of each of these studies as we continue to ponder how children learn to read. However, it is also important to consider each with a careful and critical eye toward methodology and interpretation of outcome.

Phonemic awareness. Phonemic awareness, in its simplest definition, is the ability to segment, delete, and combine speech sounds into abstract units. While children will be able to hear phonemes, they may not be able to conceptualize them as units. This concept is even more complex than this description would suggest. Phonemic awareness must be based upon a growing understanding of the alphabetic principle of English; there is sufficient evidence that many children basically understand this before they have been taught—and mastered—the set of letter-to-sound correspondences (Adams, 1990, p. 63).

Data that influence the interest in phonemic awareness (sometimes shortened to PA) include:

- Poor readers have lower phonemic awareness (Juel, 1994).

- Very young children differ in phonemic awareness (Chaney, 1992).

- Phonemic awareness can be improved by training (Ball & Blachman, 1991; Cunningham, 1990; Hatcher, Hulme, & Ellis 1994; Lundberg, Frost, & Peterson, 1988).

The research of the last decade emphasizes the absolutely critical role played by phonemic awareness in the development of the ability to decode and to read for meaning (Adams, 1990; Juel, 1988, 1991; see also pp. 40-41 in this document). The weight of evidence, irrespective of mode of instruction, suggests that phonemic awareness is a necessary but not sufficient condition for the development of decoding and reading. Allington (1997) notes that while there is a convergence of evidence emphasizing the importance of phonemic awareness in learning to read an alphabetic language, the evidence also indicates that most children (80-85 percent) acquire this awareness by the middle of first grade as a result of typical experiences at home and at school. Both Juel and Adams have documented the success of teaching phonemic awareness directly; however, they also find that it is highly likely to develop as a consequence of learning phonics, learning to read, and learning to write, especially when teachers encourage students to use invented spellings. Context appears to be critical to the efficacy of phonemic awareness as a predictor of success; the impact of increased performance in isolated phonemic awareness tasks on tests of reading comprehension is considerably less (Tumner, Herriman, & Nesdale, 1988). If, for example, a child is able to produce invented spelling in which most or all phonemes are represented, phonemic awareness has been demonstrated, thus obviating the need for any training in it.

Some students may need more explicit instruction in phonemic awareness, but in general the development of phonemic awareness in emergent readers is supported by the following:

- *Language play*: Games that emphasize rhyming, and thinking about the structure of words, particularly exploit children's tendency to first unconsciously analyze and discriminate sounds at the onset/rime level rather than the individual phonemic level.

- *Opportunities to help children notice and use letters and words*: Knowledge is further fostered through the use of alphabet centers and word walls (Fountas & Pinnell, 1996). This includes becoming familiar with letter forms, helping children learn to use visual aspects of print, providing opportunities to notice and use letters and words that are embedded in text, providing a growing inventory of known letters and words, helping children link sounds and letters and letter clusters, and helping children use what they know about words to solve new words (Adams, 1990; Cunningham, 1990; Fountas & Pinnell, 1996; Read, 1975; Schickedanz, 1986).

- *Invented spelling*: Experiences provide a medium through which both phonemic awareness and phonics knowledge develop (Adams, 1990; Clarke, 1988; Juel, 1991; Wilde, 1992; Winsor & Pearson, 1992).

- *Language experience*: Dictation of children's own oral language—in the form of stories and experiences—becomes the texts from which children read; modeling and demonstration of particular phonemic awareness and phonic knowledge occur as the teacher takes dictation (Adams, 1990; Allen, 1976).

- *Reading for meaning*: To develop such decoding proficiency, provide many models of reading aloud, of demonstrating and problem-solving using phonemic knowledge while reading aloud, providing manageable, connected texts for beginning readers to apply their phonemic awareness successfully (Gough, in Pearson, 1993).

- *Rich experiences with language, environmental print, patterned stories, and "Big Books"*: These provide a broad range of experiences to model, demonstrate, and explicitly teach phonemic awareness (Adams, 1990; Juel, 1991; Pearson, 1993).

Phonics, in general. Phonics knowledge (including but going beyond phonemic awareness) can be taught through a wide variety of methods: intensive, explicit, synthetic, analytic, embedded. All phonics instruction focuses on the learner's attention to the relationships between sounds and symbols as an important strategy for word recognition. There is little evidence that one form of phonics instruction is strongly superior to another (Stahl, McKenna, & Pagnucco, 1994).

While there is no disagreement about sound-symbol relationships as critical aspects of reading, and thus of learning to read, it is important to distinguish between the alphabetic principle of English (that is, there is a sound-symbol relationship) and the phonetic principle (that is, there is high consistency between sound and letter patterns—Spanish is phonetic but English is not). Some interesting research to consider in light of this distinction (cited in Moustafa, 1997):

- Clymer (1963) discovered that traditional phonics generalizations are not all that reliable. For example, of the 31 vowel generalizations Clymer tested, only half of them worked at least 60 percent of the time.

- Charles Read (1986) found that the "creative spelling" of four-year-olds followed particular developmental patterns that reflected their emerging knowledge and understanding of written language rules. This occurred in patterns parallel to oral language development; children recreated the general rules of the language through their approximations and interactions with sophisticated users of print (cf. Adams, 1990; Weaver, 1994 for thorough discussions).

Weaver, Gillmeister-Krause, and Vento-Zogby (1996) see four major points of agreement about the teaching of phonics even among such varying perspectives:

- Children should be given some explicit, direct help in developing phonemic awareness and a functional command of phonics.

- Such direct teaching does not need to be intensive and systematic to be effective.

- Indeed, worksheets and rote drills are not the best means of developing phonics knowledge (e.g., A. E. Cunningham, 1990).

- Phonemic awareness and phonics knowledge also develops without instruction, simply from reading and writing whole, interesting texts.

Sweet (1993) adds that it is a balance of activities designed to improve word recognition, including phonics instruction and reading meaningful text, that is necessary for creating effective beginning reading instruction.

The focus is on providing for the child what he needs when he needs it, rather than relying upon a set curriculum to meet the assumed needs of every child. No one teaching method is a panacea, as some children continue to have difficulty in developing phonemic awareness and phonics knowledge no matter how they are taught (Freppon & Dahl, 1991). However, teaching phonics knowledge in context and through discussion and collaborative activities seems to be more effective with more children than other means. Also, some studies show that children in classrooms where skills are taught in the context of reading and writing whole texts get a better start on becoming proficient and independent readers, beyond simply becoming word-callers (e.g., Freppon & Dahl, 1991; Kasten & Clark, 1989; Ribowsky, 1985; Stice & Bertrand, 1990).

What about beginning readers who struggle? Much of the research on the role of phonemic awareness and phonics instruction will point to the need for more direct, systematic, explicit teaching of this aspect of the reading process for such beginning readers (e.g., Delpit, 1986, 1988). However, there are equally substantive studies that point to the increased benefit of contextual literacy experiences—storybook reading, in particular, but also other meaningful interactions with print—to struggling readers (Purcell-Gates, McIntrye, & Freppon, 1995). At the same time, research shows that by fourth grade, the relationship between phonic knowledge and successful reading no longer shows a strong correlation (Chall, 1983). What does this imply for instruction?

Instruction for cultural, ethnic, and linguistic minority students that is primarily skills-based may limit children's learning by failing to develop their analytical skills or conceptual skills or by failing to provide purposes for learning (Knapp & Shields, 1990). Thompson, Mixon, and Serpell (1996) suggest that instructional methods for teaching reading to these children emphasize construction of meaning (Au, 1993; O'Donnell & Wood, 1992), language development (Heath, Mangiola, Schecter, & Hall, 1991; Ovando, 1993; Tharp, 1989), and higher order thinking skills, including metacognitive and prior knowledge strategies (Chamot, 1993; Crawford, 1993; Cummins, 1986; Pogrow, 1992). Delpit (1988) and Gay (1988) believe it is important to offer a "balance" within a curriculum for minority students that provides explicit instruction in "the language of power" within a meaningful context that acknowledges all students are capable of critical, higher order thinking.

Types of texts. There is much discussion now as to what types of texts are best for young children to beginning to read. Terms such as "manageable," "decodable," and "predictable" are bandied about. Allington (1997) finds there is no single well-designed study to support the exclusive use of "decodable" texts, those which contain words made up of only the phonetic sounds children have been explicitly taught. Rather, it appears that children need opportunities to engage in a variety of texts for a variety of purposes; for beginning readers, this means texts that are "manageable," i.e., those that ask children to apply their phonemic awareness and phonic knowledge in ways that support their growing sophistication, rather than challenge them to frustration. These texts will have a variety of features, including high-frequency sight words, easily decodable words, predictable story structures, and stories and/or information that are meaningful and give purpose to the reader. Teachers will also provide a variety of ways to provide support for readers as they work through such texts.

Which is best? Some helpful information:

- Early readers read print better in familiar context (e.g., in stories) than in isolation (Goodman, 1965; Kucer, 1985; Nicholson, 1991; Rhodes, 1979; Stanovich, 1991).

- Early readers also typically read stories with familiar language better than stories with unfamiliar language such as the language found in "decodable" text (Moustafa, 1997).

- The more print words children recognize, the better position they are in to make analogies between familiar and unfamiliar words to pronounce unfamiliar words (Goswami, 1986, 1988; Moustafa, 1995).

- Phonics is best learned in the context of connected, informative, engaging text (Adams, 1990).

- Children need to work with a variety of texts (e.g., fiction, nonfiction, poetry) through a variety of instructional methods (e.g., shared reading, reading aloud, guided reading, independent reading; see pp. 49-50 in this document).

10. Children learn successful reading strategies in the context of real reading.

To be effective at making meaning, readers need to learn appropriate strategies for orchestrating the information provided at all levels by the four cueing systems. Research based in miscue analysis and running records (e.g., documentation of the kinds of errors readers make and their impact on meaning-making) continues to provide insight into the kinds of strategies effective readers choose to employ (Clay, 1972; Goodman, 1965; Goodman, Watson, & Burke, 1987). This includes the use of strategic cues to construct meaning of the text via words, structures, meanings, and purposes in the text; knowing what to do before, during, and after reading a particular piece; knowledge of the similarities and differences among different text structures; and the use of self-monitoring strategies (Does it make sense? What do I do if it doesn't? What do I know that can help me to understand this text?)

Sweet (1993) describes expert readers as having strategies they use to construct meaning before, during, and after reading. Strategies are plans for solving problems they encounter in their reading experiences. A strategic reader (Paris, Lipson, & Wixson, 1983; Paris, Wasik, & Turner, 1991) is the problem solver who draws from her toolbox of metacognitive strategies to repair virtually any comprehension failure that might arise (Pearson, 1993, p. 503). Strategies that have been identified as critical to learning include (Cooper, 1993; Sweet, 1993):

- *Inferencing*: the process of reaching conclusions based on information within the text; the cornerstone of constructing meaning. Inferencing includes making predictions using prior knowledge combined with information available from text.

- *Identifying important information*: the process of finding critical facts and details in narrative (e.g., stories) or expository (e.g., informational) text. Because of text structures, the type of information to seek is different. Knowing strategies for approaching each type of text is critical to successful meaning making (Beck, Omanson, & McKeown, 1982). Good readers appear to use text structure more than poor readers (Englert & Hiebert, 1984; McGee, 1982; Myer, Brandt, & Bluth, 1980; Taylor, 1980).

- *Monitoring*: a metacognitive or self-awareness process. Efficient readers know when they have a problem, and have a variety of strategies at hand to "fix" the problem.

- *Summarizing*: a process that involves pulling together important information gathered from a long passage of text.

- *Question generating*: involves readers asking themselves questions they want answered from reading that require them to integrate information while they read (Baumann, 1984; Palincsar & Brown, 1984; Pressley, Gaskins, Wile, Cunicelli, & Sheridan, 1991; Pressley, Schuder, & Bergman, 1992; Rinehart, Stahl, & Erickson, 1986) .

When teachers model these strategies, they are treated as a set of ways for constructing meaning instead of as independent activities that are isolated from the literacy context.

Readers must learn to recognize the differences within text structures (e.g., poetry, nonfiction, narrative texts). Opportunities to interact with many types of texts, in tandem with explicit instruction in problem-solving strategies for making sense of such texts, must be provided. Reading instruction across curricular areas (e.g., science, social studies) can provide learners with an understanding of authentic uses for these strategies throughout reading experiences.

Teaching skills and strategies in the context of real reading provides students with opportunities to make sense of what they are reading as well as to experience the "how-tos" of reading within authentic purposes. Two instructional strategies that emphasize this are:

- *Story retellings*. Children have the opportunity to retell stories they have read, and to relate them to personal experiences. Teachers can use these experiences to model and demonstrate a variety of strategies (Brown & Cambourne, 1990).

- *Transactional strategies instruction* (Pressley, El-Dinary, Gaskins, Schuder, Bergman, Almasi, & Brown, 1992). Comprehension monitoring and problem-solving strategies are taught as children read real texts. Personal meanings are encouraged and personal enjoyment is emphasized.

11. Children learn best when teachers employ a variety of strategies to model and demonstrate reading knowledge, strategy, and skills.

Children need a wide variety of experiences with texts to gain sophistication in reading. In addition, teachers need to employ a wide variety of teaching strategies to provide the appropriate scaffolds for individual learners. Effective teachers of reading make instructional decisions as to how they will provide experiences and opportunities for children to learn to read. These decisions are based upon:

- The teacher's knowledge of current best practice in literacy instruction;

- The teacher's knowledge of each child's abilities and needs;

- Choices as to the type of instructional setting necessary for an experience (small group, whole group, partners, individual work); and

- Choices as to the need of implicit or explicit instruction in a particular situation.

The role of scaffolding—the careful use of guidance and support—is critical as a way for teachers to structure their instructional interactions with learners (Applebee & Langer, 1983; Bruner, 1975). Modeling as a scaffold of support can occur as part of the everyday literacy experience, for example, when reading a story aloud to children while also engaging them in the meaning of story and conveying a purpose for reading, or as an explicit modeling to demonstrate to students how to approach a task, such as how to use a table of contents (Roehler & Duffy, 1991). To be effective, such modeling practices must be seated within whole literacy events lest they easily become instances of isolated skills teaching.

Flexible patterns of grouping children are important for effective instruction (Flood, Lapp, Flood, & Nagel, 1992):

- Long-term ability grouping can create serious problems for students that are social in nature, but cognitive in effect (Allington, 1980; Barr, 1989; Hiebert, 1983; Indrisano & Parratore, 1991; Shannon, 1985).

- Supportive patterns provide a variety of opportunities for social interaction: working individually, working in cooperative groups, working in pairs or small groups to develop questions, meeting in small groups to read to each other, reading aloud to the teacher on an individualized basis, and listening as a whole group to a read-aloud piece of literature and then working individually (Au, 1991; Cunningham, Hall, & Defee, 1991).

- The most appropriate grouping pattern for each instructional experience can only be determined by analyzing student strengths and needs and matching this information with the choices available to the teacher and student. There must be a successful interaction of three sets of variables to ensure student success: (a) choosing the most appropriate basis for grouping, (b) choosing the most effective format, and (c) choosing the most appropriate materials (Flood, Lapp, Flood, & Nagel, 1992, p. 44)

What type of instructional model is appropriate? Models that implement theories—both old and new—continue to emerge within everyday classroom practice. The debate continues over the efficacy of different types of instruction, variously labeled, for example, "direct instruction," "explicit instruction," "models," and "demonstrations." Direct instruction, by itself, holds a wide variety of connotations for educators: Those trained in Special Education often equate this term with the Distar method (Gersten & Carnine, 1986), while many educators trained in current cognitive/brain-based learning theory define direct instruction as a method using cognitive strategies to directly teach students.

Much research validates the importance of explicit instruction for the processes and strategies acknowledged by current research. This strategy suggests that teachers who take the time to model, explain differences, show significance, and guide students in their acquisition can make an important impact on students' successful learning. Pearson (1996, p. xvii) clarifies the term explicit instruction: "Explicit instruction bears a family resemblance, albeit a weak one, to one of its intellectual predecessors, direct instruction, because of a common emphasis on clarity and systematicness on the presentation of skills and strategies. But the resemblance ends there.... Explicit instruction is less likely to employ skill decomposition (breaking a complex skill down into manageable pieces), which is a staple of direct instruction, as a strategy for dealing with the complexity of important strategies. Instead, it is more likely to employ 'scaffolding' as a tool for coping with complexity. Second, explicit instruction is more likely than direct instruction to rely on authentic texts rather than special instructional texts in both initial instruction and later application." Our new understandings of how we learn occasions the need to rethink our teaching strategies to move beyond traditional labels and terminology. For the purposes of this document, the term "explicit instruction" will be used, in light of Pearson's definition above.

Some researchers advocate a theory of "eclecticism" where teachers select the best teaching and learning activities from various approaches to literacy instruction as a means of meeting the diverse needs of learners. However, Rhodes and Dudley-Marling (1996) see a problem with this approach: When choosing activities regardless of their theoretical basis, teachers risk involving students in significant contradictions on the role of readers in making meaning. Eclecticism, they argue, assumes that readers learn to read "once and for all, by whatever means" (p. 28), which ignores the social aspects of literacy. Teachers must be clear, they argue, as to the assumptions they convey in regard to how people learn to read and what it means to read.

Caine and Caine (1997) contend current learning theory shows the need for a variety of teaching strategies, but most importantly, emphasizes the needs of individual students. A variety of experiences both in and out of school and a focus on critical thinking are also critical elements of emerging theories.

Teaching strategies. As teachers devise ways to effectively meet the needs of all students, they should provide a variety of opportunities for children to interact with text. Depending on the purpose and amount of guidance, an individual child will work with texts at various levels of difficulty. Fountas and Pinnell (1996, pp. 22-24) document particular kinds of teaching models and demonstrations as important for effective reading programs that include:

- *Shared reading*: Holdaway (1979) built this model upon the notion of scaffolding to give children the opportunity to practice in a supportive session the knowledge, skill, and strategy they were learning. Usually designed for use in a whole-group setting, shared reading provides many models and demonstrations within the context of real text. The teacher provides an introduction to a particular reading concept, strategy, and/or skill, often using an enlarged text. Fountas and Pinnell find that a shared reading experience explicitly demonstrates early strategies such as word by word matching; builds a sense of story and ability to predict; demonstrates processes of reading extended text; like reading aloud, involves children in an enjoyable and purposeful way; provides social support from the group; provides an opportunity to participate and behave like a reader; and creates a body of known texts that children can use for independent reading and as resources for writing and word study (Holdaway, 1979; Martinez & Roser, 1985; Pappas & Brown, 1987; Rowe, 1987; Snow, 1983; Sulzby, 1985; Teale & Sulzby, 1986).

- *Reading aloud*: Much research supports this strategy of continually modeling reading practices, and allowing children to "experience and contemplate literary work they cannot yet read" (Fountas & Pinnell, 1996, p.1). Reading aloud involves children in reading for enjoyment; demonstrates reading for a purpose; provides for an adult demonstration of phrased, fluent reading; develops a sense of story; develops knowledge of written language syntax; develops knowledge of how texts are structured; increases vocabulary; expands linguistic repertoire; supports intertextual ties; creates a community of readers through enjoyment and shared knowledge; makes complex ideas available to children; promotes oral language development; and establishes known texts to use as a basis for writing and other activities through rereading (Adams, 1990; Clark, 1976; Cochran-Smith, 1984; Cohen, 1968; Durkin, 1966; Goodman, Y., 1984; Green & Harker, 1982; Hiebert, 1983; Ninio, 1980; Pappas & Brown, 1987; Schickedanz, 1978; Wells, 1986).

- *Oral reading*: In traditional methodology, "round robin" reading where each child takes a turn reading the same text is still a commonly observed practice although many have been critical of such practices (Taubenheim & Christensen, 1978; Taylor & Connor, 1982; True, 1979). There are several reasons cited as to why group oral reading is often not the best choice, including the lack of provision for opportunities for a great deal of reading of a complete text (Allington, 1980; Hoffman, 1981) and lack of the development of effective, efficient, and independent reading strategies. Also, round robin reading often interferes with comprehension development because of the focus upon correctly pronouncing the words; this is particularly true for poor readers (Hoffman, 1981; Winkeljohann & Gallant, 1979).

  Oral reading is best seen as a "practice" strategy for beginning readers, and as a way to monitor their growth and development during a running record or a miscue analysis. Teachers can provide a variety of oral reading opportunities for students that enhance their reading development: reading with a buddy, pausing during the reading of a piece to discuss and orally rereading parts that pertain to the discussion, involving children in shared reading experiences, and holding individual conferences with students. With practice, oral reading can provide readers with an avenue for performance (e.g., dramatization of stories, reader's theater, reading aloud to others) and response.

- *Guided reading*: Usually designed for use with small groups of children, guided reading provides a setting where teachers can focus in on reading strategies for particular children as they evolve into independent readers. This teaching strategy provides the opportunity to read a wide variety of texts, to problem solve while reading for meaning, to use strategies on extended text, and to attend to words in text. In addition, guided reading challenges the reader and creates context for successful processing on novel texts; and makes teacher selection of text, guidance, demonstration, and explanation available to the reader (Clay, 1991a, 1991b; Holdaway, 1979; Lyons, Pinnell, & DeFord, 1993; McKenzie, 1986; Meek, 1988; Routman, 1991; Wong, Groth, & O'Flahavan, 1994). Guided reading offers teachers specific opportunities to model and show readers particular aspects of the reading process. It gives children the opportunity to develop as individual readers while participating in a socially supported activity and gives teachers ongoing opportunities to observe individuals as they process new texts (cf. Clay, 1991a; Fountas & Pinnell, 1996).

- *Individual (independent) reading*: This provides opportunities to apply reading strategies independently; provides time for sustained reading behavior; challenges the reader to work on his/her own and to use strategies on a variety of texts; challenges the reader to solve words independently while reading texts well within his/her control; promotes fluency through rereading; builds confidence through sustained, successful reading; and provides the opportunity for children to support each other while reading (Clay, 1991a; Holdaway, 1979; McKenzie, 1986; Meek, 1988; Taylor, 1983).

Learning goals.

- *Fluency*. Successful readers are fluent readers: That is, they are able to rapidly and smoothly process text in what appears to be an effortless construction of meaning. While some believe that automaticity (Samuels, 1994)—the ability to quickly decode words—is the critical aspect of fluency, others believe fluency to be a complex interrelationship of processes that allows the reader to flexibly, rapidly, and often without conscious attention access information while also focusing on gaining meaning from the text (Clay, 1991a). It is possible that becoming a fluent reader has as much to do with meaning construction as it has to do with attending to the words on a page (Pinnell, Pikulski, Wixson, Campbell, Gough, & Beatty, 1995). Fluency does vary with the type and difficulty of a text; those fluent also know how to change the rate of reading to meet the needs of their transaction between the text and the reader. It is thus impossible to become consistently fluent with every kind of text. An important goal, then, is for students to gain an increasingly wider range of reading situations in which they are fluent. It is important to note:

- Oral reading fluency has a significant relationship with reading comprehension. The results of the NAEP Integrated Reading Performance Record assessment suggests reading fluency may have as much to do with gaining meaning from text as it does with being highly accurate with words (Pinnell, et al., 1995). In comparison, the relationship between accuracy and overall fluency appeared to be much weaker.

- Oral reading fluency appears to be related to the access to and interaction with a wide variety of literacy experiences, including the use of libraries and other activities outside of school (Pinnell, et al., 1995). Fluent reading may be, in part, a result of frequent practice in reading (Anderson, Wilson, & Fielding, 1988; Watkins & Edwards, 1992).

- Accuracy, rate, and fluency were interrelated in some ways: Pinnell, et al., 1995, found highly accurate performance did not necessarily guarantee highly fluent reading; this is also true to some extent for reading rate.

- Fluency appears to be more than simply a sum of its parts (Pinnell, et al.,1995, p. 52). Reading accurately, while important, is not sufficient for supporting fluent reading. Fluent readers must be able to utilize an awareness of syntax, phrasing, and expression that undoubtedly goes beyond simply being able to read words.

- A lack of fluency in reading could be situated in several interrelated sources including the student's perception that reading is the correct recognition of words, the student's fear of taking risks in the process of reading, and the student's store of knowledge about reading as language (Harste & Burke, 1980).

- Miscue research demonstrates that there is often no difference in the use of graphophonics by proficient and nonproficient readers; rather, the difference is found in their use of syntax and semantics in conjunction with graphophonics (Cambourne & Rousch, 1982; Goodman, Watson, & Burke, 1987; Pflaum & Bryan, 1982). The limited store of information about reading of nonproficient readers can also limit their fluency.

- Students' perceptions about reading impact reading performance (Harste & Burke, 1980). Helping students to understand their own perceptions of what reading is and what good readers do is a critical step in moving them toward more fluent reading.

- *Discussion and response to text*. The context within which any teaching strategy is employed is critical to its success. Given that reading is a socially constructed event, carried out via interactions with others within a particular social group, the discussions involved in response to any text are vital to students' success as readers.

Those who participate in discussions are active learners who engage in the construction of knowledge (Gambrell, 1996). Thus, the primary goal of instruction through discussion is to help students construct personal meanings in response to new experiences rather than to simply learn the meanings others have created (Poplin, 1988). Discussions—of ideas generated by the reading as well as ideas generated about the process of reading—support learning through the social interactions of students to construct knowledge.

When students are encouraged to verbalize their ideas and questions, cognitive development is supported. They learn how to realize uncertainties in their understandings, explain and justify their positions, seek information to help them resolve the uncertainty, and learn to see alternative points of view (Almasi, 1995; Brown & Palincsar, 1989; Doise & Mugny, 1984; Johnson & Johnson, 1979; Mugny & Doise, 1978). Student interaction in discussions promotes the ability to think critically and to consider multiple perspectives (Almasi, 1995; Green & Wallet, 1981; Hudgins & Edelman, 1986; Prawat, 1989; Villaume & Hopkins, 1995) and develops the ability to confirm, extend, and modify their individual interpretations of texts (Eeds & Wells, 1989; Leal, 1992). Discussion promotes deep understanding of text (Eeds & Wells, 1989; Morrow & Smith, 1990; Palincsar, 1987; Palincsar & Brown, 1984).

Students who talk about what they read are more likely to be motivated to read (Guthrie, Schafer, Wang, & Afflerbach, 1995; Morrow & Weinstein, 1986). Student participation in discussions increases self-esteem while fostering positive attitudes, quality communication skills, and friendships among students of different backgrounds (Almasi, 1995; Eeds & Wells, 1989; Goatley & Raphael, 1992; Philips, 1973; Slavin, 1990). The quality of the discourse in discussions is more complex than the dialogue of students who participate in more traditional teacher-led recitations (Alamasi, 1995; Eeds & Wells, 1989; Leal, 1992; Sweigart, 1991).

Response to literature through discussion can be implemented in a variety of ways. Group discussions of texts are influenced by:

- *text type* (Leal, 1992; Horowitz & Freeman, 1995).

- *group size*. Small group is preferable—large enough to ensure diversity of ideas, yet small enough so that each student has an opportunity to fully participate (Davidson, 1985; Morrow & Smith, 1990; Palincsar, Brown, & Martin, 1987; Rogers, 1991; Sweigert, 1991; Wiencek & O'Flavahan, 1994).

- *leadership*. Clearly, students profit from their own agendas during discussion; however, it appears that they also profit from teacher guidance. Teachers play a significant role in guiding students toward higher level discussions as they engage in modeling behavior, providing frameworks for approaching texts, and posing interpretive questions (McGee, 1992; O'Flahavan, Stein, Wiencek, & Marks, 1992).

- *the cultural background of the participants* (Heath, 1983; White, 1990). Learning focusing on cooperation and interaction has been found to be highly effective in improving achievement among African American children (Strickland & Ascher, 1992), native Hawaiian children, and Hispanics (Wong Fillmore & Meyer, 1992).

Formats include:

- Pair students with a "buddy" to interact and problem solve. Discussions become more productive as students gain in social skills.

- Form a cooperative learning group of students with varying abilities to read, discuss, or respond to a piece of text. More formal approaches include literature circles (Short, Harste, & Burke, 1996) and Book Clubs (Raphael & McMahon, 1994).

- Use story retellings as a beginning framework for discussion of texts. This is particularly successful for children who come from cultures with a rich oral tradition (Thompson, Mixon, & Serpell, 1996).

- Whenever possible, use the discussion structure of the prominent culture in discussions of texts. For example, Au (1993) uses the Hawaiian "talk-story" structure to provide native Hawaiian students with a familiar discussion format.

Written response to what is read is also important. Writing provides important scaffolds and models for children as they write about their thoughts, feelings, and ideas. Students can document what they have read and their responses to it in literature logs. Following simple formats, young children can compose important artifacts of their growing sophistication as readers. In addition, children can respond to reading through drama, dance, and art.

- *Questioning*. Questioning, once thought of as a hierarchical set of levels through which to move, is now viewed as a complex cognitive process. Not only is it important for teachers to move students—even those at early and emergent stages of reading—beyond literal levels of recall to levels of synthesis, evaluation, comparison/contrast, and problem solving. Students must also learn to ask a wide variety of questions, rather than to simply look for details within a text. Questions, rethinking, and refined understandings result when students discuss their understandings of themes or concepts that appear in a text (Langer, 1991).

Formats include:

- Question Answer Relationships (QARs) (Raphael, 1986). Children are given clues to help them find information in the text and in their head. Because of its specificity, Thompson, Mixon, and Serpell (1996) suggest this for culturally diverse students.

- reciprocal teaching (Palincsar & Brown, 1984). Children take turns in pairs asking questions about and summarizing pieces of text. Gradually, they work independently from the teacher. This strategy improves engagement, comprehension, and cognitive processing.

12. Children need the opportunity to read, read, read.

Access, time, modeling, choice, multiple readings, difficulty: All of these are factors in providing children with many opportunities to read (Allington, 1977, 1980; Allington & Cunningham, 1996; Stanovich, 1986). What is critical is that children do read—lots, for sustained periods of time, for meaning, and for real and authentic purposes. Pearson (1993, pp. 507-508) observes: "One is tempted to conclude that some of the best 'practice' for enhancing reading skill occurs when students are given greater opportunity to read everyday materials."

The effect of opportunity to read on various measures of reading skill or achievement shows:

- "Just plain reading" improves students' comprehension (Anderson, Wilson, & Fielding, 1988); vocabulary knowledge (Herman, Anderson, Pearson, & Nagy, 1987); ability to monitor their own reading for sense (Pinnell, 1989); disposition to read independently (Ingham, 1982); and English grammar skills (Elley & Mangubhai, 1983).

- There is a consistently positive relationship between the amount of voluntary reading completed at home or at school and gains on standardized reading achievement tests (Pearson & Fielding, 1991).

One focus of reading instruction is to develop the lifelong habit of reading. Holdaway (1979), however, points out that schools spend a great deal of time teaching literacy skills, then leave little room for children to practice those skills by really reading. Why is the success of most reading programs gauged by the "successful" scores on standardized reading tests rather than by the personal reading habits of their students (Irving, 1980; Spiegel, 1981)? If instructional programs do not provide ample opportunity for students to read for enjoyment in school, desire and motivation to do so may not develop (Lamme, 1976; Speigel, 1981). When students are held accountable for a wide variety of reading experiences (e.g., compiling reading logs, participating in sustained silent reading, documenting reading at home experiences), positive attitudes toward reading will develop.

Libraries. Krashen (1993, 1995) has found a critical relationship between access to books via public and school libraries and reading achievement. Indicators of school library quality and public library use were found to be significant predictors of reading comprehension scores. Allington and Cunningham (1996) also emphasize this relationship. The national trend of shrinking library funding is particularly hard on low-income areas; schools enrolling many poor children have 50 percent fewer books than do schools enrolling primarily more advantaged students (Guice & Allington, 1994). Some suggest that very broad national differences in literacy are related to the per capita amount of print available to the average adult (Guthrie & Greaney, 1991). (cf. Pearson, 1993, pp. 507-508; Pearson & Fielding, 1991).

To best support children, books need to be available through both classroom collections and schoolwide libraries. Classroom libraries give students immediate access, a factor likely to increase the amount of voluntary reading students do in and out of school (Fractor, Woodruff, Martinez, & Teale, 1993). Schools serving many at-risk students need particularly good collections in both places because these children typically have much less access out of school. Because of their critical importance in providing students with materials to read, Allington and Cunningham (1996) recommend the urgent need for library collections and services to expand.

Ways to provide wide opportunities for voluntary reading:

- Schedule at least one block of structured sustained silent reading for students each day (SSR, DEAR, etc.). Have children document what they read, and give opportunities to talk about what they have read. Time varies: Fifteen minutes for kindergartners is usually appropriate, with increased time as students' abilities and attention spans develop.

- Model your own pleasure reading during sustained silent reading time. Resist the urge to use this time to work with students, correct papers, write letters, make phone calls, or balance your checkbook.

- Provide a varied collection of print material in your classroom: library books, personal books, student-written books; newspapers (community, city, regional); magazines (for children, community based); brochures and pamphlets of interest to the children in your room; menus and other such environmental print.

- Provide an opportunity for all children to acquire a library card. Many public libraries have programs that work closely with public schools to make their services accessible to all children.

- Create book bag programs for children to take home classroom/school materials to read with families. These programs usually include opportunities for families and children to respond to the reading in some fashion, and to document the reading time spent.

13. Monitoring the development of reading processes is vital to student success.

Monitoring learners' progress calls for a variety of assessment and evaluation strategies. Assessment and instruction are integral processes, each informing the other to meet the individual needs of students. Teachers must constantly use keen observation of student growth and development to inform instruction. Also, students must learn to become critically aware of their own reading processes, that is, to become metacognitive, to facilitate their development as meaningful, fluent readers. Evaluation, on the other hand, takes into account all assessments and observations in order to make a judgment about an individual student for grading and/or placement purposes.

Traditional modes of monitoring development have occurred via standardized/norm-referenced instruments and criterion-referenced tests. While these measures show where an individual falls within a peer group, they do not necessarily show in detail what an individual can do as a reader. Some drawbacks to traditional modes (Allington & Walmsley, 1995) include:

1. They are largely unreliable bases for making any judgments about an individual's reading development.

2. They rarely have much demonstrated validity as they assess only a narrow range of literacy activity.

3. They are given infrequently and at odd times of the year so the results, even if reliable and valid, are not of much use in planning and instruction.

4. They tend to narrow the curriculum as teachers feel the need to "teach the test"; some see this as working to discourage teacher-learner collaborative evaluation of literacy learning.

5. They can play a role in discouraging those children whose performance on the tests suggests that their reading development lags behind that of their peers (pp. 78-79; Darling-Hammond, 1991; Stallman & Pearson, 1990).

Standardized tests will likely remain an important aspect of school literacy programs. However, many standardized tests are being revised to incorporate current definitions of reading. Currently, there are many examples of strategies for monitoring and assessing reading development that incorporate the research developments of the past 25 years, including comprehension monitoring (cognitive development), response to texts beyond a literal level (cognitive development, response theory), errors as ways of indicating knowledge (language acquisition, emergent literacy), strategy use, and attitude. Many reform efforts highlight the need for "performance" assessments: That is, are learners able to actually translate and apply skills and strategies in new, authentic tasks? What do learners do? The impact of research can be seen in both informal, classroom-level assessments and more formal, standardized kinds of assessments.

For example, the most current NAEP reading assessment (Mullis, Campbell, & Farstrup, 1992; Williams, Reese, Campbell, Mazzeo, & Phillips, 1995) reflected this trend toward performance-based assessments grounded in current theories of reading. The construction of this assessment was based upon the general agreement of educators defining literacy learning as occurring through a broad range of oral and written activities including personally meaningful experiences (such as responding to reading), reflection on reading, interacting with others about reading, and choosing to read independently (Ruddell & Ruddell, 1994). Tasks required students to construct, extend, and examine meaning while reading a variety of texts for a variety of purposes (Pinnell, Pikulski, Wixson, Campbell, Gough, & Beatty, 1995, p. 4).

Current understandings of how children learn to read suggest the following assessment recommendations: assess authentic reading and writing in texts that make all cue systems available to students; assess reading in a variety of contexts and situations; assess products as well as processes; use multiple sources of data to find patterns in student growth and development; involve all involved with the student in the assessment process (students, parents, school personnel); and make assessment an ongoing part of everyday reading and writing tasks (Rhodes & Dudley-Marling, 1996). Developmental patterns and behavior in reading and writing are based upon current research (Cochrane, Cochrane, Scalena, & Buchanan,1984; Holdaway, 1979) as well as on standards for reading as presented by national organizations (IRA/NCTE, 1996), state departments of education (Commission on Student Learning, 1996), and local districts.

Aspects of reading development to monitor.

- *Personal perceptions, attitudes, and interests.* Students' personal perceptions are impacted by their attitudes, beliefs, and interests. Comprehension of texts is always influenced by social and historical values and expectations, both known and unknown. These perceptions help teachers to understand how individuals socially situate the act of reading: How is time spent with reading? Who is involved in conversations about reading? The importance of reading, and the sense of one's of ability to read, will affect the choices students make in regard to reading, including types and time of reading.

   Ways to document personal perceptions, attitudes, and interests include:

   - *interviews* to provide insight into individual perceptions. Teachers can construct their own interviews or use Burke's Reading Interview (Goodman, Watson, & Burke, 1987), which focuses on perceptions of what reading is and what good readers do. Rhodes and Dudley-Marling (1996) also emphasize the particular importance for at-risk readers to gain insight into their own beliefs and perceptions of the reading process, and their interactions with this process.

   - *inventories* to help teachers to find out about students' interests and connections to reading in and out of school. This might include inventories of the number of books read and owned at home as well as reading logs of what is read at school.

   - *observation* of how students interact in a variety of situations that require reading. How does this individual interact with others in regard to reading and books? What choices do individuals make in regard to reading?

   - *anecdotal records* of individual background information that might be helpful in understanding how reading is socially situated.

- *Comprehension.* The meaning made by readers is at the heart of the reading process. How is background knowledge used in constructing meaning? What kind of sense is made of the texts read? What comprehension strategies (e.g. predicting, skimming, rereading) are used in order to construct meaning? Is the appropriate literary knowledge in place to apply to understand this text (e.g., story structure, formats, literary elements, genres, and particular authors)?

Ways to document comprehension include:

- *response*: Responding to texts in a variety of ways helps children to demonstrate a synthesis of what they have gained from interaction with their own lives. How does it apply to their own lives? What sense can they make of the text? How does this compare and contrast to other texts they have read? This may happen through writing in literature logs, through a dramatic presentation, by discussing the book in a literature discussion group with peers, or by book talks as a way to convince others to read the book.

- *retelling*: Brown and Cambourne (1990) and Goodman, Watson, and Burke, (1987) encourage teachers to use forms of retelling to get at what students understand about the content of stories read as well as their structure. Retelling is a way of getting to students' comprehension of what has been read. It is an assessment/monitoring strategy as well as a teaching strategy.

- *Informal Reading Inventory (IRI)/Qualitative Reading Inventory (QRI)*: These inventories provide normed assessments that focus on children's comprehension of text. The QRI, in particular, incorporates elements of miscue analysis and retelling in its procedures (Leslie & Caldwell, 1990).

- *interviews*: These can used to find out what students have gained through their reading of a text.

- *observations*: Teachers can watch as students read, asking questions and keeping anecdotal records.

- *Processing words and other text features*. How students process words and other text features has an integral relationship with their comprehension and understanding of a text. There is probably the most debate about how to view instruction at the word level, and thus of how to best assess and monitor the development of students' ability in this area.

At one level, it is important for students to understand the concepts of letters, of word, and of sentence. Marie Clay's (1972, 1991, 1993) work with children at the emergent stage of literacy development highlights the importance of monitoring the development of concepts about print. Clay highlights the importance of presenting these tasks in ways as authentic and meaningful as possible.

Ways to document the processing of words and text features include:

- *concepts of print*: Children are interviewed, with a book, about directionality (Where is the front of this book? Where do I begin to read? Where do I go from here?), and about their concepts of letters and words (Show me one letter; Show me two letters; Show me a word; Show me a sentence). Clay's (1972) *Sand* and *Stones* texts provide a structured format from which to assess these concepts.

- *identification of letter names and sounds*: Children point to and tell letter names and sounds they know. At emergent levels, this focuses on single letter names and sounds, but can move to more sophisticated groupings of letters (blends and digraphs) as they are introduced and taught to children.

- *word knowledge*: Children are asked to read familiar words (usually high frequency words with which they have some interaction).

- *writing*: Children are asked to write whatever they would like. Teachers observe how children go about this task: How do they perceive writing? What types of symbols do they choose to use? What does their attempt say about their knowledge of phonemic awareness and phonic knowledge?

- *hearing and recording sounds in words*: Children write a dictated sentence. Teachers analyze their response by counting the representation of sounds by letters.

Some believe it is important to continue to document children's phonemic awareness; that is, how able are they to discriminate and segment letter sounds in speech (e.g., c-a-t). Often, this can be observed in the context of daily classroom experiences by clapping syllables, observing the growth of invented spelling, and work with rhyming words.

At another level, it is important to look at how readers process words and text features within the meaningful context of a text. What kinds of errors (miscues) do readers make? How do these miscues seem to affect comprehension? What do the miscues reveal about the strategies and cues they use to process text? Do students use other text features to comprehend text?

Ways to do this include:

- *error analysis/miscue analysis*: Research in miscue analysis (Goodman, Watson, & Burke, 1987) and running records (Clay, 1972, 1991, 1993) has provided teachers with important insights into how children read, as well as with important tools for documenting reading behaviors of children. All readers make errors; it is through analysis of these errors that intent and strategy can be determined. Oral reading of a text is an important avenue through which teachers can observe reading behaviors (Pinnell, et al., 1995). Clay (1991) highlights the importance of a reader's use of language patterns and text structures in successful reading; error analysis can help teachers to understand the thought processes and problem-solving strategies readers use and do not use. There are many formats to follow for this assessment (Clay, 1993; Goodman, Watson, & Burke, 1987; Rhodes, 1993). In general, students read an unfamiliar text, providing a retelling when they have finished. Teachers record their miscues, analyzing them to discover the strategies used and the ability of the reader to make sense of the text.

- *anecdotal records and observation*: Teachers must carefully watch what readers are doing and continue to record these observations for analysis over time.

    – *student self-assessment*: Within a structure and set of expectations provided by the teacher, students reflect upon their abilities (What am I able to do well? What have I learned to do?) and set new personal goals (What is an appropriate next step for me?).

- *Metacognitive strategies*. Students who are able to think and talk about the strategies they use are better able to draw upon their own resources to problem solve as they encounter difficulties in their reading, "thinking about their thinking" as they go about a task. Students need to be able to understand when, how, and why they are applying particular reading strategies and skills, and what might be important to help them progress in their development.

Ways to document this include:

    – *think-alouds*: Thinking aloud as a text is read gives insight into the strategies readers are using. Teachers can gauge why comprehension is or is not occurring as they listen to what strategy choices the reader is making (Brown & Lytle, 1988).

    – *student self assessment*: Given a set of expectations, students reflect upon their ability to use metacognitive strategies and set new goals as appropriate.

    – *interviews*: Teachers interview students as to what they do as they read. This often occurs as students are reading a text.

    – *anecdotal records and observation*: Teachers observe and record what they see students doing as they read.

- *Environment and instruction*. Reading is a transaction between the reader, the text, and the environment within which they rest. It is appropriate to move assessment beyond what is perceived to be "in" a student. Home, school, and community environments all contribute to literacy development.

Ways to document this relationship include:

    – *teacher self-assessment and reflection*: Teachers must reflect upon the matches necessary among the classroom environment, instructional decisions, and the needs of individual students. When students do not appear to be succeeding, teachers consider why this is so from as many perspectives as possible. What factors might be an obstacle for students? What alternatives might be employed?

    – *student self assessment and reflection*: As students reflect upon their own learning, insights into obstacles and issues can provide new options for instruction.

Recently, the incorporation of student portfolios as a means of gathering and monitoring reading development has gained in favor as performance-based assessments have been developed. Portfolios offer ways to include multiple measures taken over time of an individual's reading as documentation.

Conclusion

There are, in the end, only two main ways human beings learn, by observing others (directly or vicariously) and by trying things out for themselves. Novices learn from experts or experience. That's all there is to it. Everything else is in the details (Deborah Meier, 1995, Center for Collaborative Education).

What Helps Children Learn to Read?

Location, location, location: the "three" factors to consider in buying a house. Can we reduce the complex body of research knowledge presented here, even our 13 core understandings about learning to read, to a single, powerful mantra? We think we can:

Learning to read is about access.

Access is key. In both oral language acquisition and learning to read, access is the critical component. Children with access to rich and responsive language interactions about their experiences in the first three years of life develop power over language even as they learn to talk. Their orientation to the world around them is one of agency and curiosity. They acquire ever larger vocabularies as they notice, talk about, and receive adult feedback on experiences. These children come to school ready to continue that quest for knowledge and to make their own the words that name it.

In the same way, children learning to read need access to meaningful and personally interesting texts. This opens another way of learning about the world to them. And since background knowledge and experience are so important to reading comprehension, the more children are reading, the more they increase the grounding they bring to the next text...and the next. They increase their "world knowledge" even as they are acquiring "word knowledge" (Allington & Cunningham, 1996).

The motivation to read builds as the child finds meaning in texts, and the child follows a trajectory much like s/he did in learning to talk: Increased engagement in the process fuels learning, positive disposition, and control of skills and strategies. Juel (1992) found the differences in achievement between poor and good first-grade readers were remarkably consistent, even though all the children were making gains. She believes that the critical factor was the amount of reading children actually did, i.e., their access to real encounters with books. First-graders who were good readers read approximately twice as many words during the year as did poor readers. This pattern held fast through fourth grade. Reading frequently and widely is essential for reading achievement. For struggling readers more time for real reading is imperative if we are ever to narrow this gap.

To say that children learn to read by reading is not to deny the need to provide explicit instruction and many demonstrations in the classroom. The point to be made is that the amount of extended text reading that children do is directly related to their reading achievement. Without real engagement with meaningful texts, children will not become readers. This is why a focus on early instruction in isolated skills is potentially so damaging for young readers, especially those who struggle to learn to read.

Specifically, children learning to read need access to:

- Time for reading and learning

- Texts of all kinds and rich resources for learning to read

- Knowledgeable and supportive teachers

- Appropriate instruction in skills and strategies

- Demonstrations of how readers, writers, and texts work

- Other readers, both novice and expert

- Their own reading processes

Providing access to these critical components in the classroom.

- *Time*: Children need to have sustained periods of engagement with texts (blocks of time in the school day with plenty of time for guided reading, independent reading, work with words, talking about books). Children need time to grow to love reading and to choose it for both learning and pleasure.

- *Texts and resources*: Classrooms and schools need richly stocked libraries that offer children information and enjoyment, representing the many cultures and perspectives of our diverse society. Included in the school's resources must be books of all sorts as well as electronic texts and literacy applications, including computers with high quality reading software, integrated media technology, and the Internet (Sharp, Bransford, Goldman, Kinzer, & Soraci, 1992). As children are learning to read, they need "lots of easy stuff to read" (Allington & Cunningham, 1996). Trained librarians work closely with teachers to keep the media center collection current and are available to put just the right resource in a child's hands. Children's access to quality school library media centers, staffed by professionals, has a direct correlation with reading achievement and with positive attitudes about reading (Routman, 1996).

- *Knowledgeable and supportive teachers*: Teachers must thoroughly understand current theories of language, literacy, and learning. This understanding must be demonstrated in and enhanced by their classroom practice. It is vitally important that teachers see themselves as lifelong learners, always updating their practitioner knowledge, and for this reason institutional structures to nurture teachers' professional development are essential. Schools need to be seen as places where teachers learn, too. But knowledge is not enough for teachers of reading.

In addition, they must communicate both high expectations for children's learning and the assurance of their support for each child to succeed. The desire to learn to read and write is powerfully affected by teacher expectations, the patience and caring of the teacher, and the quality of communication that motivates and engages students in the learning process (Rosenholtz, 1989). Joan Yatvin, a superintendent of a rural district in Oregon, writes:

> In order to learn, a child must believe: I am a learner; I can do this work; craftsmanship and effort will pay off for me; this is a community of friends, and I belong to it. Because such beliefs often are not the inherent property of children who come from splintered families and dangerous neighborhoods, teachers today must work as hard on them as they have always worked on the intellectual side of learning (1992, p. 7).

- *Appropriate instruction*: This, too, is the responsibility of the teacher. Excellent teachers of reading establish regular literacy routines that provide opportunities for children to work independently, in small groups and as a whole class (see Core Understanding #11). It should be noted, though, that a reliance on whole-class instruction for reading is not good, because it distances teachers from children's development as readers (Allington & McGill-Franzen, 1997). Teachers need to know how individual children are progressing, what understandings of literacy they are developing. Teachers need to work closely with children to know what a child needs right then to support his/her next steps as a reader. Classrooms should be organized to provide children access to the teacher, time, each other, books, etc. that they need to be successful in learning to read.

In becoming readers, all children must develop the same understandings, i.e., the ability to use all four of the cueing systems to construct meaning with text. But children will not all need the same amount or kind of instruction in all the systems. Providing instruction that is responsive to the child's needs is key. Children who require more explicit instruction in any aspect of reading will understandably need more time. One way teachers meet this need is the use of flexible groups as part of their literacy routines. The best resources for skill and strategy instruction in such groups are real texts, e.g., trade books (fiction and nonfiction) and children's writing.

James Baumann (1997) recommends that while literacy instruction activities should be enjoyable, it's also important to acknowledge to children that learning to read is hard work. Children need to be taught how to "read words and puzzle out texts." Furthermore, children need to experience the power of strenuous effort as they grapple with sometimes difficult material (Carnegie Corporation, 1996).

- *Demonstrations of how readers, writers, and texts work*: Children need to see lots of examples of how readers and writers work and of how reading and writing are used for various purposes. Reading aloud to children is a powerful way to demonstrate not only how books work, but also to model a love for reading. One important use of reading is as a learning tool; young readers need to see how it works this way. As students are involved in whole class, small group, paired, and individual literacy activities these demonstrations are provided and used by readers of varying degrees of expertise.

Furthermore, classroom experiences and instruction that integrate reading, writing, speaking, and listening support literacy development because they keep the language picture whole. Talking and writing in response to reading, listening to stories, writing original stories all feed "the linguistic data pool" described in Section II (Brown & Cambourne, 1990; Harste, Burke, & Woodward, 1983) . Basically, reading, and writing, listening, and speaking are streams that flow into the same pool; they are constantly refreshing each other, if our classrooms take advantage of their complementarity.

- *Other readers*: Some children are surrounded by readers in their home and community, adults who share books with them from their earliest years. As Bernice Cullinan notes (cited in Putnam, 1994), "Children who sit beside a reader and follow the print from an early age learn to read quite 'naturally.' We know that the modeling has a lasting effect; children do what they see others do" (p. 363). But children who come to school without rich reading experiences at home need access not only to books but to skilled readers who will envelop them in the language and experience of books. Sometimes the reader will be the teacher, sometimes another adult from the school or the community, sometimes an older student. The important thing is that children experience the support of a skilled reader to help them bond with books.

  Children also need to talk with each other about what they are reading. They learn about books they would like to read, sharpen their own understandings of a text by listening to others' responses, and become a community of readers.

- *Their own reading processes*: Children's awareness of what they know and can do as readers is essential to their literacy growth. The goal of Reading Recovery is to foster a "self-extending system of literacy expertise," developed as the child reads more and consciously acquires and applies an ever-widening repertoire of reading strategies (Clay, 1991, p. 317). As with all of Reading Recovery's interventions for struggling readers, this goal is derived from careful observation of what good readers do. The title of one of Clay's recent books (1991) says it all—*Becoming Literate: The Construction of Inner Control*.

Research on learning to high levels of literacy points out important cognitive strategies which children must develop and consciously implement, including (a) problem-solving or fix-up strategies, (b) self-regulatory procedures, (c) "executive structures" or goals and purposes for reading, and (d) intentional learning procedures (Dreher & Slater, 1992). Ongoing instruction and assessment should involve children in setting such goals and monitoring progress toward them.

What Can Hinder Children in Learning to Read?

Basically, classroom practices that isolate skills from meaningful reading make learning to read difficult. They do not help children develop this inner control and strategic functioning as readers. Years ago, Frank Smith published a widely circulated essay entitled, "Twelve Easy Ways to Make Learning to Read Difficult, and One Difficult Way to Make It Easy." Smith's 12 ways were all variations on a theme of distancing the child from his/her attempts to read for meaning. However well intentioned, these instructional approaches denied the child access to reading as a meaning-making process. In contrast, the simple but elegant prescription for how to make learning to read easy was to "respond to what the child is trying to do" (1973, p. 24).

At the 1997 International Reading Association Convention in Atlanta, Georgia, reading researchers from across the pedagogical spectrum participated in a symposium that shared research revisiting and updating Smith's propositions (Flippo, 1997). The symposium, Reaching Consensus in Literacy Education: Beginnings of Professional and Political Unity, presented the points of agreement among participants on practices which help children become readers and those which make learning to read difficult. The practices which they agreed on as helpful are all incorporated in the discussion above. The practices which they agreed would hinder effective reading development are listed below:

- Emphasizing only phonics

- Drilling on isolated letters or sounds

- Teaching letters and words one at a time

- Insisting on correctness

- Expecting students to spell correctly all the words they can read

- Making perfect oral reading the goal of reading instruction

- Focusing on skills rather than interpretation and comprehension

- Constant use of workbooks and worksheets

- Fixed ability grouping

- Blind adherence to a basal program

Of course, the phrasing of some of the practices suggests why agreement across the spectrum was possible, e.g., "emphasizing only," "drilling," "focusing on," and "blind adherence." Nevertheless, the pressure from some quarters today to make explicit, systematic phonics the core of reading instruction in the primary grades, and to define reading as decoding, could lead to valuable classroom time being used for the very practices soundly rejected by these reading experts. Children could lose access to the rich resources and interactions that prompt engagements with reading, outlined in the 13 core understandings.

Roles and Responsibilities: Supporting All Children to Reach High Levels of Literacy

Our challenge, to bring all children to the critical/translation level of literacy described by Myers (1996), is daunting. At the same time that our standards for literacy are rising, some children in our schools struggle to acquire basic skills in reading and our school populations are more diverse than ever before. How can we meet the varied needs of individual children and help them all develop a firm command of basic skills and strategies, the ability to construct and negotiate meanings with text, the knowledge and the disposition to be critical, lifelong readers? As policymakers, educators, parents—adults involved in children's education—we all have significant roles to play.

"Effective classroom teachers are the only absolutely essential element of an effective school," assert Allington and Cunningham (1996, p. 81). They go on to suggest that the usefulness of all professionals in the school—administrators, specialists (Title I, special education, talented and gifted), librarians, social workers, ESL/bilingual teachers, school psychologists—should be judged by the impact they have on enhancing the quality of classroom instruction. For children who experience difficulty learning to read, the focus on delivering high-quality, consistent classroom instruction is especially important. They cannot afford a fragmented or confused message about reading.

Ensuring excellent classroom instruction will take collaboration among professional staff, initially to agree upon goals for the literacy program and then to develop shared understandings of effective literacy practices. This may mean that staff members undertake a program of learning for themselves, possibly in a reading and study group or through action research on some aspect of their literacy program.

Since we know that students' reading achievement is directly related to the amount of reading they do, building support with parents for reading at home is very important. And while independent reading is a goal, reading with children and talking about books is also necessary. Not only does talking about books motivate children to read, it enhances their development of important cognitive strategies. In fact, classroom studies are showing that social interaction as well as strategy instruction is strongly related to the amount and breadth of students' reading (Guthrie, Schafer, Wang, & Afflerbach, 1995).

The final point to be made is the importance of a supportive, united community of adults as the child learns to read. The school can take the leadership in welcoming parents and community members into the schools, building bridges between home and school literacy, providing access to rich literacy materials, and offering appropriate training or strategy information for parents and volunteers. Children learning to read need adults who support them to be on the same page: understanding that reading is a construction of meaning.

BIBLIOGRAPHY

Introduction

Adams, M. J. (1990). *Beginning to read: Thinking and learning about print*. Cambridge, MA: The MIT Press.

Allen, J., Michalove, B., & Shockley, B. (1993). *Engaging children: Community and chaos in the lives of young literacy learners*. Portsmouth, NH: Heinemann.

Allington, R., & Cunningham, P. (1996). *Schools that work: Where all children read and write*. New York, NY: Harper Collins.

Anderson, T., & West, K. (1995). An analysis of qualitative investigations: A matter of whether to believe (Commentary). *Reading Research Quarterly, 30*(3), 562-569.

Atwell, N. (1987). *In the middle*. Portsmouth, NH: Boynton/Cook, Heinemann.

Baker, L., Afflerbach, P., & Reinking, D. (1996). *Developing engaged readers in school and home communities*. Mahwah, NJ: Lawrence Erlbaum Associates.

Boyer, E. (1995). *The basic school: A community for learning*. Princeton, NJ: The Carnegie Foundation for the Advancement of Teaching.

Caine, R., & Caine, G. (1991). *Making connections: Teaching and the human brain*. Alexandria, VA: Association for Supervision and Curriculum Development.

Carnegie Corporation of New York (1994, April). Starting points: Meeting the needs of our youngest children. *The report of the Carnegie Task Force on Meeting the Needs of Young Children*. New York, NY: Author.

Carnegie Corporation of New York (1996, September). Years of promise: A comprehensive learning strategy for America's children. *The report of the Carnegie Task Force on Learning in the Primary Grades*. New York, NY: Author.

Clay, M. M. (1991). Becoming literate: *The construction of inner control*. Portsmouth, NH: Heinemann.

Collier, V. (1995, Fall). Acquiring a second language for school. *Directions in Language and Education, National Clearinghouse for Bilingual Education, 1*(4), 1-10.

Commission on Student Learning. (1996, January). *Essential academic learning requirements: Reading, writing, communication and mathematics*. Olympia, WA: Author.

Edelsky, C. (1990). Whose agenda is this anyway? A response to McKenna, Robinson, and Miller. *Educational Researcher, 19*(8), 7-11.

Introduction (continued)

Eisenhart, M. (1995). Whither credibility on research in reading: A response to Anderson and West. *Reading Research Quarterly, 30*(3), 570-572.

Elliott, E. (1996). Literacy: From policy to practice. *Journal of Literacy Research, 28*(2), 452-457.

Freeman, D., & Freeman, Y. Re: Celt reply: Two views of reading research [Online]. Available e-mail: lewisjp@plu.edu from yfreeman@fresno.edu, April 10, 1997.

Freire, P. (1970). *Pedagogy of the oppressed* (M. B. Ramos, Trans.). New York, NY: Herder & Herder.

Glesne, C., & Peshkin, A. (1992). *Becoming qualitative researchers.* New York, NY: Longman.

Goodman, K. (1965). A linguistic study of cues and miscues in reading. *Elementary English, 42*, 639-643.

Goodman, Y. (1976). Strategies for comprehension. In P. Allen & D. Watson (Eds.), *Findings of research in miscue analysis: Classroom implications* (pp. 94-102). Urbana, IL: ERIC Clearinghouse on Reading and Communication Skills & National Council of Teachers of English.

Graves, D. (1981). *A case study observing the development of primary children's composing, spelling, and motor behaviors during the writing process* (Final report) (NIE grant no. G-78-0174). Durham, NH: University of New Hampshire. (ERIC Document Reproduction Service No. 218 653)

Graves, M., van den Broek, P., & Taylor, B. (Eds.). (1996). *The first R: Every child's right to read.* New York, NY: Teachers College Press.

Green, J., & Dixon, C. (1996). Language of literacy dialogues: Facing the future or reproducing the past. *Journal of Literacy Research, 28*(2), 290-301.

Guthrie, J. (1997, January). The director's corner. *NRRC News: A Newsletter of the National Reading Research Center*, p. 3.

Hart, B., & Risley, T. (1995). *Meaningful differences in the everyday experience of young American children.* Baltimore, MD: Paul H. Brookes.

Healy, J. (1990). *Endangered minds: Why children don't think and what we can do about it.* New York, NY: Touchstone Books.

Hiebert, E. (Ed.). (1991). *Literacy for a diverse society: Perspectives, practices, and policies.* New York, NY: Teachers College Press.

Introduction (continued)

International Reading Association & National Council of Teachers of English (1996). *Standards for the English language arts*. Newark, DE: International Reading Association & Urbana, IL: National Council of Teachers of English.

International Reading Association (1997, January). *The role of phonics in reading instruction* (A position statement of the International Reading Association). Newark, DE: International Reading Association.

Lytle, S. & Cochrane-Smith, S. L. (1992). Teacher research as a way of knowing. *Harvard Educational Review, 52*(4), 447-474.

McKenna, M. C., Robinson, R. D., & Miller, J. W. (1990). Whole language: A research agenda for the nineties. *Educational Researcher, 19*(8), 3-6.

Michigan Department of Education. (1989). *Michigan Department of Education reading assessment review process*. Lansing, MI: Author.

Morrow, L.M. (1996). *Motivating reading and writing in diverse classrooms: Social and physical contexts in a literature-based program* (Research report no. 28). Urbana, IL: National Council of Teachers of English.

Mosenthal, P. (1995). Why there are no dialogues among the divided: The problem of solipsistic agendas in literacy research. *Reading Research Quarterly, 30*(3), 574-577.

Mullis, I., Campbell, J., & Farstrup, A. (1993). *Executive summary of the NAEP 1992 reading report card for the nation and the states: Data from the national and trial state assessments*. Washington, DC: National Center for Education Statistics.

Myers, J. (1995). The value-laden assumptions of our interpretive practices. *Reading Research Quarterly, 30*(3), 582-587.

Myers, M. (1996). *Changing our minds: Negotiating English and literacy*. Urbana, IL: National Council of Teachers of English.

National Center for Education Statistics (1995, October). *NAEP 1994 reading: A first look. Findings from the National Assessment of Educational Progress*. Washington, DC: Author.

Nieto, S. (1997, Summer). Participant in Ethnicity and Education forum: What difference does difference make? *Harvard Education Review, 67*(2), 169-187.

Pace, G. (1993). *Making decisions about grouping in language arts* (Literacy Improvement Series for Elementary Educators, Literacy, Language and Communication Program). Portland, OR: Northwest Regional Educational Laboratory.

Introduction (continued)

Patterson, L., & Shannon, P. (1993). Reflection, inquiry, action. In L. Patterson, C. Santa, K. Short, & K. Smith (Eds), *Teachers are researchers: Reflection in action* (pp. 7-11). Newark, DE: International Reading Association.

Pearson, P., & Stephens, D. (1994). Learning about literacy: A 30 year journey. In R. Ruddell, M. Ruddell, & H. Singer (Eds.), *Theoretical models and processes of reading* (4th ed., pp. 22-42). Newark, DE: International Reading Association.

Pearson, P. D. (1996). Six ideas in search of a champion: What policymakers should know about the teaching and learning of literacy in our schools. *Journal of Literacy Research, 28*(4), 302-309.

Purcell-Gates, V. (1997, April). Focus on research: The future of research in language arts. *Language Arts, 74*, 280-283.

Roehler, L. (1997, May 5-9). *Reaching consensus in literacy education: Beginnings of professional and political unity* (Symposium participant). Presentation at the International Reading Association Annual Convention, Atlanta, 1997.

Shanahan, T., & Neuman, S. (1997). Conversations: Literacy research that makes a difference. *Reading Research Quarterly, 32*(2), 202-211.

Shockley, B., Michalove, B., & Allen, J. (1995). *Engaging families: Connecting home and school literacy communities.* Portsmouth, NH: Heinemann.

Sticht, T. G., Caylor, J. S., Kern, R. P., & Fox, L. C. (1972). Project REALISTIC: Determination of adult functional literacy skill levels. *Reading Research Quarterly, 7,* 424-465.

Sweet, A. (1993, November). *State of the art: Transforming ideas for teaching and learning to read.* Washington, DC: U.S. Department of Education, Office of Educational Research and Improvement.

Taylor, D. (1993). *From the child's point of view.* Portsmouth, NH: Heinemann.

Weaver, C. (1994). *Reading process and practice: From socio-psycholinguistics to whole language,* 2nd edition. Portsmouth, NH: Heinemann.

Acquiring Language: Basic Understandings

Applebee, A., & Langer, J. (1983). Instructional scaffolding: Reading and writing as natural activities. *Language Arts, 60*, 168-175.

Bissex, G. (1980). *GNYS AT WRK: A child learns to write and read.* Cambridge, MA: Harvard University Press.

Bloom, B. (1985). *Developing talent in young people.* New York, NY: Ballantine Books.

Acquiring Language: Basic Understandings (continued)

Brown, R. (1973). *A first language: The early stages.* Cambridge, MA: Harvard University Press.

Brown, H., & Cambourne, B. (1990). *Read and retell.* Portsmouth, NH: Heinemann Educational Books.

Brown, R., Cazden, C., & Bellugi-Klima, U. (1968). The child's grammar from one to three. In J. P. Hill (Ed.), *Minnesota symposium on child development.* Minneapolis, MN: University of Minnesota Press.

Bruner, J. (1975). The ontogenesis of speech acts. *Journal of Child Language, 3,* 1-19.

Caine, R.N., & Caine, G. (1991). *Making connections: Teaching and the human brain.* Alexandria, VA: Association for Supervision and Curriculum Development.

Caine, R.N., & Caine, G. (1997). *Education on the edge of possibility.* Alexandria, VA: Association for Supervision and Curriculum Development.

Cambourne, B. (1988). *The whole story: Natural learning and the acquisition of literacy in the classroom.* Auckland, New Zealand: Ashton Scholastic.

Carnegie Corporation of New York. (April, 1994). Starting points: Meeting the needs of our youngest children. *The report of the Carnegie Task Force on Meeting the Needs of Young Children.* New York, NY: Author.

Cazden, D. (1988). *Classroom discourse: The language of teaching and learning.* Portsmouth, NH: Heinemann.

Chafe, W., & Danielwicz, J. (1986). Properties of spoken and written language. In R. Horowitz & S.J. Samuels (Eds.), *Comprehending oral and written language.* New York, NY: Academic.

Chomsky, N. (1959). A review of B.F. Skinner's *Verbal Behavior. Language, 35*(1), 26-58.

Chomsky, N. (1965). *Aspects of the theory of syntax.* Cambridge, MA: MIT Press.

Clark, R. (1983). *Family life and school achievement: Why poor black children succeed or fail.* Chicago, IL: University of Chicago Press.

Clay, M. (1966). *Emergent reading behavior* (Doctoral dissertation, University of Auckland, New Zealand, 1966).

Clay, M. (1972). *The early detection of reading difficulties: A diagnostic survey with recovery procedures.* Exeter, NH: Heinemann.

Clay, M. (1977). *What did I write?* Exeter, NH: Heinemann Educational Books.

Acquiring Language: Basic Understandings (continued)

Cochran-Smith, M. (1984). *The making of a reader*. Norwood, NJ: Ablex.

Dahl, K.L., & Freppon, P.A. (1995). A comparison of innercity children's interpretations of reading and writing instruction in the early grades in skills-based and whole language classrooms. *Reading Research Quarterly, 30*(1), 50-74.

Edwards, P. (1989). Supporting lower SES mothers' attempts to provide scaffolding for bookreading. In J. Allen & J. Mason (Eds.), *Risk makers, risk takers, risk breakers: Reducing the risks for young literacy learners*. Portsmouth, NH: Heinemann.

Edwards, P. (1991). Fostering early literacy through parent coaching. In E. Hiebert (Ed.), *Literacy for a diverse society: Perspectives, practices, and policies*. New York, NY: Teachers College Press.

Ferreiro, E., & Teberosky, A. (1982). *Literacy before schooling*. Exeter, NH: Heinemann.

Goodman, Y. (1984). The development of initial literacy. In H. Goelman, A. Oberg, & F. Smith (Eds.), *Awakening to literacy*. Exeter, NH: Heinemann.

Halliday, M.A.K. (1973). *Explorations in the functions of language*. London, United Kingdom: Edward Arnold.

Halliday, M.A.K. (1975). *Learning how to mean: Exploration in the development of language*. London, United Kingdom: Edward Arnold.

Harste, J. C., Burke, C.L. & Woodward, V.A.. (1983). Children's initial encounters with print, N.I.E. Grant proposal, cited in Hardt, V.H. (ed.) *Teaching reading with the other language arts*. Newark, DE: International Reading Association, p. 44

Harste, J., Woodward, V., & Burke, C. (1984). *Language stories and literacy lessons*. Exeter, NH: Heinemann.

Hart, B., & Risley, T. (1995). *Meaningful differences in the everyday experience of young American children*. Baltimore, MD: Paul H. Brookes.

Heath, S.B. (1982). What no bedtime story means. *Language in Society, 11*, 49-76.

Heath, S.B. (1983). *Ways with words*. Cambridge, United Kingdom: Cambridge University Press.

Holdaway, D. (1979). *The foundations of literacy*. Sydney, Australia: Ashton Scholastic.

Krater, J., Zeni, J., & Cason, N. (1994). *Mirror images: Teaching writing in black and white*. Portsmouth, NH: Heinemann Educational Books.

Leichter, H. (1984). Families as environments for literacy. In H. Goelman, A. Oberg, & F. Smith (Eds.), *Awakening to literacy*. Exeter, NH: Heinemann.

Acquiring Language: Basic Understandings (continued)

Mason, J. (1980). When do children begin to read? An exploration of four-year-old children's letter and word reading competencies. *Reading Research Quarterly, 15*, 203-227.

Mason, J. (1992). Reading stories to preliterate children: A proposed connection to reading. In P. B. Gough, L. C. Ehri, & R. Treiman (Eds.), *Reading Acquisition.* Hillsdale, NJ: Erlbaum.

Morrow, L. M. (1978). Analysis of syntax in the language of six-, seven-, and eight-year-olds. *Research in the Teaching of English, 12*, 143-148.

Morrow, L. M. (1996). Motivating reading and writing in diverse classrooms: Social and physical contexts in a literature-based program (Research Report No. 28). Urbana, IL: National Council of Teachers of English.

Morrow, L. M. (1997). *Literacy development in the early years: Helping children read and write* (3rd ed.). Boston, MA: Allyn and Bacon.

Morrow, L. M., O'Connor, E., & Smith, J. (1990). Effects of a story reading program on the literacy development of at-risk kindergarten children. *Journal of Reading Behavior, 20*(2), 104-141.

Moustafa, M. (1997). *Beyond traditional phonics: Research discoveries and reading instruction.* Portsmouth, NH: Heinemann.

Neuman, S., & Roskos, K. (1992). Literary objects as cultural play: Effects on children's literacy behaviors in play. *Reading Research Quarterly, 27*(3), 202-225.

Ninio, A. (1980). Picturebook reading in mother-infant dyads belonging to two subgroups in Israel. *Child Development, 51*, 587-590.

Ninio, A., & Bruner, J. (1978). The achievement and antecedents of labeling. *Journal of Child Language, 5*, 1-6.

Olson, D.R. (1977). From utterance to text: The bias of language in speech and writing. *Harvard Educational Review, 47*, 257-281.

Pace, G. (1993). *Making decisions about grouping in language arts.* Portland, OR: Northwest Regional Educational Laboratory.

Piaget, J., & Inhelder, B. (1969). *The psychology of the child.* New York: Basic Books.

Pinnell, G. S. (1985). Ways to look at the functions of children's language. In A. Jaggar & M. T. Smith-Burke (Eds.), *Observing the Language Learner.* Newark, DE: International Reading Association.

Purcell-Gates, V. (1988). Lexical and syntactic knowledge of written narrative held by well-read-to kindergartners and second graders. *Research in the Teaching of English, 22,* 128-160.

Purcell-Gates, V., McIntyre, E., & Freppon, P. (1995). Learning written storybook language in school: A comparison of low-SES children in skills-based and whole language classrooms. *American Educational Research Journal, 32*(3), 659-685.

Read, C. (1975). Children's categorization of speech sounds in English (National Research Report No. 17). Urbana, IL: National Council of Teachers of English.

Rubin, A. D. (1978). A theoretical taxonomy of the differences between oral and written language (Technical Report No. 35). Urbana, IL: University of Illinois, Center for the Study of Reading.

Smith, F. (1971). *Understanding reading.* New York, NY: CBS College Publishing.

Sulzby, E. (1985). Children's emergent reading favorite storybooks. *Reading Research Quarterly, 20,* 458-481.

Sulzby, E. (1986). Writing and reading: Signs of oral and written language organization in the young child. In W. Teale & E. Sulzby (Eds.), *Emergent literacy: Writing and reading.* Norwood, NJ: Ablex.

Tannen, D. (1982). *Spoken and written language: Exploring orality and literacy. Vol IX: Advances in discourse processes.* Norwood, NJ: Ablex.

Taylor, D. (1983). *Family literacy: Young children learn to read and write.* Exeter, NH: Heinemann.

Taylor, D., & Strickland, D. (1986). *Family storybook reading.* Portsmouth, NH: Heinemann.

Teale, W. (1978). Positive environments for learning to read: What studies of early readers tell us. *Language Arts, 55,* 922-932.

Teale, W. (1982). Toward a theory of how children learn to read and write naturally. *Language Arts, 59,* 555-570.

Teale, W. (1986). The beginning of reading and writing: Written language development during the preschool and kindergarten years. In M. Sampson (Ed.), *The pursuit of literacy: Early reading and writing.* Dubuque, IA: Kendall-Hunt.

Vygotsky, L. S. (1978). *Mind in society: The development of psychological processes.* Cambridge, MA: Harvard University Press.

Wells, G. (1986). *The meaning makers.* Portsmouth, NH: Heinemann.

Factors that Influence Literacy Learning

Ada, A. F. (1980). No one learns to read twice: The transferability of reading skills. *Aides to Bilingual Education Report, 1*(1). Washington, DC: ACW.

Adams, M. (1990). *Beginning to read: Thinking and learning about print.* Cambridge, MA: The MIT Press.

Allington, R. (1977). If they don't read much, how they ever gonna get good? *Journal of Reading, 21,* 57-61.

Allington, R. (1980). Poor readers don't get to read much in reading groups. *Language Arts, 5*(8), 873-875.

Allington, R. (1983). The reading instruction provided readers of differing abilities. *Elementary School Journal, 83,* 548-559.

Allington, R. (1994a). What's special about special programs for at-risk kids? *Journal of Reading Behavior, 26,* 1-21.

Allington, R. (1994b). The schools we have. The schools we need. *The Reading Teacher, 48,* 14-29.

Allington, R. (n.d.). Effective literacy instruction for at-risk children. In M. Knapp & P. Shields (Eds.), *Better schooling for the children of poverty: Alternatives to conventional wisdom.* Berkeley, CA: McCutchan Publishing Corporation.

Allington, R., & Cunningham, P. (1996). *Schools that work.* New York: Harper Collins.

Allington, R., & McGill-Franzen, A. (1989). School response to reading failure: Chapter 1 and special education students in grades 2, 4, & 8. *Elementary School Journal, 89,* 529-542.

Allington, R., & Walmsley, S., (Eds.). (1995). *No quick fix: Rethinking literacy programs in America's elementary schools.* Newark, DE: International Reading Association.

Au, K., & Mason, J. (1981). Social organization factors in learning to read: The balance of rights hypothesis. *Reading Research Quarterly, 17*(1), 115-152.

Au, K., & Mason, J. (1983). Cultural congruence in classroom participation structures: Achieving a balance of rights. *Discourse Processes, 6*(2), 145-167.

August, D., & Hakuta, K. (Eds.). (1997). *Improving schooling for language-minority children: A research agenda.* Washington, DC: National Academy Press.

Berko Gleason, J. (1993). *The development of language* (3rd ed.). New York, NY: Macmillan.

Factors that Influence Literacy Learning (continued)

Bialystock, E. (Ed.). (1991). *Language processing in bilingual children*. Cambridge, United Kingdom: Cambridge University Press.

Bialystock, E. (1997). Effects of bilingualism and biliteracy on children's emerging concepts of print. *Developmental Psychology, 33*(3), 429-440.

Cardenas, J., Robledo, M., & Waggoner, D. (1988). *The undereducation of American youth*. (ERIC Document Reproduction Service No. ED 309 201)

Carnegie Corporation of New York. (1996, September). Years of promise: A comprehensive learning strategy for America's children. *The report of the Carnegie Task Force on Learning in the Primary Grades*. New York, NY: Author.

Carnine, D., & Grossen, B. (1993). Phonics instruction comparing research and practice. *Teaching Exceptional Children, 25*(2), 22-25.

Clay, M. (1972). *The early detection of reading difficulties: A diagnostic survey with recovery procedures*. Exeter, NH: Heinemann.

Clay, M. (1993). *An observation survey of early literacy achievement*. Portsmouth, NH: Heinemann Educational Books.

Chavkin, N. (1989). Debunking the myth about minority parents and the school. *Educational Horizons, 67*, 119-123.

Collier, V. (1989). How long? A synthesis of research on academic achievement in second language. *TESOL Quarterly, 23*, 509-531.

Collier, V. (1992). A synthesis of studies examining long-term language minority student data on academic achievement. *Bilingual Research Journal, 16*(1-2), 187-212.

Collier, V. (1995). Acquiring a second language for school. *Directions in Language & Education: National Clearinghouse for Bilingual Education, 1*(4), 1-10.

Comer, J. (1986). Parent participation in the schools. *Phi Delta Kappan, 67*, 442-446.

Cuevas, J. (1997). *Educating limited-English proficient students: A review of the research on school programs and classroom practices*. San Francisco, CA: WestEd.

Cummins, J. (1981). The role of primary language development in promoting educational success for language minority students. In *Schooling and language minority students: A theoretical framework* (pp. 16-62). Sacramento, CA: California Department of Education. (ERIC Document Reproduction Service No.249 773)

Deford, D., Lyons, C., & Pinnell, G. (Eds.). (1991). *Bridges to learning: Learning from Reading Recovery*. Portsmouth, NH: Heinemann Educational Books.

Factors that Influence Literacy Learning (continued)

Delpit, L. D. (1986). Skills and other dilemmas of a progressive Black educator. *Harvard Educational Review, 56,* 379-385.

Delpit, L. D. (1988). The silenced dialogue: Power and pedagogy in educating other people's children. *Harvard Educational Review, 58,* 280-298.

Diaz, S., Moll, L., & Mehan, H. (1986). Sociocultural resources in instruction: A context specific approach. In California State Department of Education, *Beyond language: Social and cultural factors in schooling language minority children.* California State University, Los Angeles, CA: Evaluation, Dissemination, and Assessment Center.

Durkin, D. (1978). What classroom observations reveal about reading comprehension. *Reading Research Quarterly, 14*(4), 481-533.

Dyson, A.H. (1997). *What difference does difference make? Teacher reflections on diversity, literacy, and the urban primary school.* Urbana, IL: National Council of Teachers of English.

Edwards, P. (1989). Supporting lower SES mothers' attempts to provide scaffolding for bookreading. In J. Allen & J. Mason (Eds.), *Risk makers, risk takers, risk breakers: Reducing the risks for young literacy learners.* Portsmouth, NH: Heinemann.

Edwards, P. (1991). Fostering early literacy through parent coaching. In E. Hiebert (Ed.), *Literacy for a diverse society: Perspectives, practices, and policies.* New York, NY: Teachers College Press.

Ellis, R. (1985). *Understanding second language acquisition.* Oxford, United Kingdom: Oxford University Press.

Erickson, F. (1993). Transformation and school success: The politics and culture of educational achievement. In E. Jacob & C. Jordan (Eds.), *Minority Education: Anthropological perspectives.* Norwood, NJ: Ablex.

Erickson, F., & Mohatt, G. (1982). Cultural organization of participation structures in two classrooms of Indian students. In G. Spindler (Ed.), *Doing the ethnography of schooling: Educational anthropology in action.* New York, NY: Holt, Rinehart, & Winston.

Gallimore, R., Boggs, J., & Jordan, C. (1974). *Culture, behavior, and education: A study of Hawaiian-Americans.* Beverly Hills, CA: Sage Publications.

Gallimore, R., & Goldenberg, C. (1989). *Action research to increase Hispanic students' exposure to meaningful text: A focus on reading and content area instruction* (Final Report to the Presidential Grants for School Improvement Committee, University of California). Berkeley, CA: University of California.

Factors that Influence Literacy Learning (continued)

Garcia, E. (1994). *Understanding and meeting the challenge of student cultural diversity.* Boston, MA: Houghton Mifflin.

Gay, G. (1988). Designing relevant curricula for diverse learners. *Education and Urban Society, 20*(4), 327-340.

Garcia, P., & Nagy, S. K. (1993). English as a second language for the workplace: Worker education curriculum guide. Chicago: Northeastern Illinois University Chicago Teachers Center.

Genesee, F. (1987). *Learning through two languages: Studies of immersion and bilingual education.* Cambridge, MA: Newbury House.

Genesee, F. (Ed.). (1994). *Educating second language children: The whole child, the whole curriculum, the whole community.* Cambridge, MA: Cambridge University Press.

Goldenberg, C. (1987). Low-income Hispanic parents' contributions to their first-grade children's word-recognition skills. *Anthropology & Education Quarterly, 18*, 149-179.

Goldenberg, C., & Gallimore, R. (1991). Local knowledge, research knowledge, and educational change: A case study of first-grade Spanish reading improvement. *Educational Researcher, 20*(8), 2-14.

Goldenberg, C., & Sullivan, J. (1994). *Making change happen in a language-minority school: A search for coherence* (Educational Practice Report #13). Washington, DC: Center for Applied Linguistics.

Goodman, K., Goodman, Y., & Flores, B. (1979). *Reading in the bilingual classroom: Literacy and biliteracy.* Rosslyn, VA: National Clearinghouse for Bilingual Education.

Grossen, B., & Carnine, D. (1990). Translating research on initial reading instruction into classroom practice. *Interchanges, 21*(4), 15-23.

Hall, N. (1987). *The emergence of literacy.* Portsmouth, NH: Heinemann Educational Books.

Hakuta, K. (1986). *Mirror of language: The debate on bilingualism.* New York, NY: Basic Books.

Haynes, M., & Jenkins, J. (1986). Reading instruction in special education resource rooms. *American Educational Research Journal, 23*, 161-190.

Heath, S. B. (1983). *Ways with words.* Cambridge, United Kingdom: Cambridge University Press.

Factors that Influence Literacy Learning (continued)

Hiebert, E. (1983). An examination of ability grouping for reading instruction. *Reading Research Quarterly. 18,* 231-55.

Hudelson, S. (1987). The role of native language literacy in the education of language minority children. *Language Arts, 64*(8), 827-841.

Janopoulos, M. (1986). The relationship of pleasure reading and second language writing proficiency. *TESOL Quarterly, 20*(4), 763-768.

Jordan, C. (1984). Cultural compatibility and the education of ethnic minority children. *Educational Research Quarterly, 8*(4), 59-71.

Jordan, C. (1992). The role of culture in minority school achievement. *The Kamehemeha Journal of Education, 3*(2), 53-67.

Jordan, C. (1995). Creating cultures of schooling: Historical and conceptual background of the KEEP/Rough Rock Collaboration. *Bilingual Research Journal, 19*(1), 83-100.

Juel, C. (1994). *Learning to read and write in one elementary school.* New York, NY: Springer-Verlag.

Kozol, J. (1991). *Savage inequalities: Children in America's schools.* New York, NY: Crown Publishers.

Krashen, S. (1981). *Second language acquisition and second language learning.* Oxford, United Kingdom: Pergamon Press.

Krashen, S. (1982). *Principles and practice in second language acquisition.* New York, NY: Pergamon Press.

Krashen, S., & Terrell, T. (1983). *The natural approach: Language acquisition in the classroom.* Englewood Cliffs, NJ: Alemany Press, Regents, & Prentice Hall.

Larrivee, B. (1985). *Effective teaching for successful mainstreaming.* New York: Longman.

Lindfors, J. (1987). *Children's language and learning* (2nd ed.) Englewood Cliffs, NJ: Prentice-Hall.

Lyons, C.A. (1989). Reading recovery: An effective early intervention program that can prevent mislabeling children as learning disabled. *ERS Spectrum, 7,* 3-9.

McDermott, R. (1987). The explanation of school failure, again. *Anthropology & Education Quarterly, 18*(4), 361-364.

Mace-Matluck, B. (1982). *Literacy instruction in bilingual settings: A synthesis of current research* (Professional Papers M-1). Los Alamitos, CA: National Center for Bilingual Research. (ERIC Document Reproduction Service No. ED 222 079)

Factors that Influence Literacy Learning (continued)

Mason, J. (1986). *Use of little books at home: A minimal intervention strategy that fosters early reading* (Technical Report No. 388). Urbana, IL: Illinois University Center for Study of Reading.

Michaels, S. (1981). Sharing time: Children's narrative style and differential access to literacy. *Language in Society, 10*, 423-442.

Moll, L. (1988). Key issues in teaching Latino students. *Language Arts, 65*(5), 465-472.

Moll, L. (1992). Bilingual classroom studies and community analysis: Some recent trends. *Educational Researcher, 21*(8), 20-24.

Moll, L. (n.d.). Social and instructional issues in literacy instruction for "disadvantaged" students. In M. Knapp & P. Shields (Eds.), *Better schooling for the children of poverty: Alternatives to conventional wisdom.* Berkeley, CA: McCutchan Publishing Corporation.

Moll, L., & Diaz, S. (1987). Change as the goal of educational research. *Anthropology & Education Quarterly, 18*(4), 300-311.

Morrow, L. M. (1996). *Motivating reading and writing in diverse classrooms: Social and physical contexts in a literature-based program* (Research Report No. 28). Urbana, IL: National Council of Teachers of English.

Moss, M., & Puma, M. (1995). *The congressionally mandated study of educational growth and opportunity.* Cambridge, MA; ABT Associates, Inc. (ERIC Document Reproduction Service No. ED 394 334)

Ogbu, J. (1981). School ethnography: A multilevel approach. *Anthropology & Education Quarterly, 12*(1), 3-29.

Ogbu, J. (1990). Minority status and literacy in comparative perspective. *Daedalus, 119*(2), 141-168.

Ogbu, J. (1993). Variability in minority school performance: A problem in search of an explanation. In E. Jacob & C. Jordan (Eds.), *Minority education: Anthropological perspectives.* Norwood, NJ: Ablex.

Philips, S. (1983). *The invisible culture.* New York, NY: Longman.

Purcell-Gates, V., McIntyre, E., & Freppon, P. (1995). Learning written storybook language in school: A comparison of low-SES children in skills-based and whole language classrooms. *American Educational Research Journal, 32*(3), 659-685.

Rhodes, L., & Dudley-Marling, C. (1996). *Readers and writers with a difference: A holistic approach to teaching struggling readers and writers* (2nd ed.). Portsmouth, NH: Heinemann Educational Books.

Factors that Influence Literacy Learning (continued)

Roberts, C. (1994). Transferring literacy skills from L1 to L2: From theory to practice. *The Journal of Educational Issues of Language Minority Students, 13,* 209-221.

Roller, C. (1996). *Variability not disability: Struggling readers in a workshop classroom.* Newark, DE: International Reading Association.

Snow, C. (1992). Perspectives on second-language development: Implications for bilingual education. *Educational Researcher, 21*(2), 16-19.

Snow, C., Barnes, W., Chandler, J., Goodman, J., & Hemphill, L. (1991). *Unfulfilled expectations: Home and school influences on literacy.* Cambridge, MA: Harvard University Press.

Spear-Swerling, L., & Sternberg, R. (1996). *Off track: When poor readers become "learning disabled."* New York, NY: Westview Press.

Stanovich, K. (1986). Matthew effects in reading: Some consequences of individual differences in the acquisition of literacy. *Reading Research Quarterly, 21,* 360-407.

Street, B. (1995). *School literacies: Critical approaches to literacy in development, ethnography, and education* (Real Language Series). New York, NY: Longman.

Taylor, D. (1983). *Family literacy: Young children learn to read and write.* Exeter, NH: Heinemann.

Taylor, D., & Dorsey-Gaines, C. (1988). *Growing up literate.* Portsmouth, NH: Heinemann.

Teale, W. (1981). Parents reading to their children: What we know and what we need to know. *Language Arts, 58,* 902-911.

Teale, W. (1987). Emergent literacy: Reading and writing development in early childhood. In J. Readance & R. Baldwin (Eds.), *Thirty-sixth Yearbook of the National Reading Conference.* Rochester, NY: National Reading Conference.

Thomas, W. P., & Collier, V. T. (1997). *School effectiveness for language minority students.* National Clearinghouse for Bilingual Education.

Vanecko, J., Ames, N., & Archambault, F. (1980). *Who benefits from federal education dollars?* Cambridge, MA: ABT Books.

Wells, G. (1986). *The meaning makers.* Portsmouth, NH: Heinemann.

Learning to Read: Core Understandings

1. Reading is a construction of meaning from written text. It is an active, cognitive, and affective process.

Halliday, M.A.K. (1973). *Explorations in the functions of language.* London, United Kingdom: Edward Arnold.

Halliday, M.A.K. (1975). *Learning how to mean: Exploration in the development of language.* London, United Kingdom: Edward Arnold.

Pearson, P. D., Roehler, L. R., Dole, J. A., & Duffy, G. G. (1990). *Developing expertise in reading comprehension: What should be taught? How should it be taught?* (Technical Report No. 512). Champaign, IL: Center for the Study of Reading.

Rosenblatt, L. (1938/1976). *Literature as exploration.* New York, NY: Modern Language Association.

Rosenblatt, L. (1978). *The reader, the text, and the poem: The transactional theory of literary work.* Carbondale, IL: Southern Illinois University Press.

2. Background knowledge and prior experience are critical to the reading process.

Allington, R., & Cunningham, P. (1996). *Schools that work.* New York, NY: Harper Collins.

Anderson, R. C., & Pearson, P. D. (1984). A schema-theoretic view of basic processes in reading comprehension. In P. D. Pearson, R. Barr, M. Kamil, & P. Mosenthal (Eds.), *Handbook of reading research, vol. 1.* White Plains, NY: Longman Publishing Group.

Beck, I. L., Omanson, R. C., & McKeown, M. G. (1982). An instructional redesign of reading lessons: Effects on comprehension. *Reading Research Quarterly 17*(4), 462-481.

Clay, M. (1972). *The early detection of reading difficulties: A diagnostic survey with recovery procedures.* Exeter, NH: Heinemann.

Moustafa, M. (1997). *Beyond traditional phonics: How children learn to read and how you can help them.* Portsmouth, NH: Heinemann.

Roberts, C. (1994). Transferring literacy skills from L1 to L2: From theory to practice. *The Journal of Educational Issues of Language Minority Students, 13,* 209-221.

Rumelhart, D. E. (1980). Schemata: The building blocks of cognition. In R. J. Spiro, B. C. Bruce, & W. F. Brewer (Eds.), *Theoretical issues in reading comprehension.* Hillsdale, NJ: Lawrence E. Erlbaum Associates, Inc.

Sweet, A. (1993, November). *State of the art: Transforming ideas for teaching and learning to read.* Washington, DC: U.S. Department of Education, Office of Educational Research and Improvement.

3. Social interaction is essential in learning to read.

Applebee, A. N., & Langer, J. A. (1983). Instructional scaffolding: Reading and writing as natural activities. *Language Arts, 60*, 168-175.

Baker, L., & Brown, A. (1984). Cognitive monitoring in reading. In J. Flood (Ed.), *Understanding reading comprehension*. Newark, DE: International Reading Association.

Bruner, J. (1975). The ontogenesis of speech acts. *Journal of Child Language, 3*, 1-19.

Eeds, M., & Wells, D. (1989). Grand conversations: An exploration of meaning construction in literature study groups. *Research in the Teaching of English 23*, 4-29.

Goldenberg, C. (1993). Instructional conversations: Promoting comprehension through discussion. *The Reading Teacher, 46*(4), 316-326.

Langer, J. (1991). Discussion as exploration: Literature and the horizon of possibilities. In G. Newell & R. Durst (Eds.), *The role of discussion and writing in the teaching and learning of literature*. Norwood, MA: Christopher Gordon Publishers.

Sweet, A. (1993, November). *State of the art: Transforming ideas for teaching and learning to read*. Washington, DC: U.S. Department of Education, Office of Educational Research and Improvement.

Vygotsky, L. S. (1978). *Mind in society: The development of psychological processes*. Cambridge, MA: Harvard University Press.

Walker, B. (1996). Discussions that focus on strategies and self-assessment. In L. Gambrell & J. Almasi (Eds.), *Lively discussions! Fostering engaged reading*. Newark, DE: International Reading Association.

4. Reading and writing develop together.

Clarke, L. K. (1988). Invented versus traditional spelling in first graders' writings: Effects on learning to spell and read. *Research in the Teaching of English 22*, 281-309.

Clay, M. (1977). *What did I write?* Exeter, NH: Heinemann Educational Books.

Langer, J. A. (1986). Reading, writing, and understanding: An analysis of the construction of meaning. *Written Communication 3*(2), 219-267.

Pearson, P. D., & Tierney, R. J. (1984). On becoming a thoughtful reader: Learning to read like a writer. In A. C. Purves & O. Niles (Eds.), *Becoming readers in a complex society. Eighty-third yearbook of the National Society of the Study of Education*. Chicago, IL: University of Chicago Press.

Squire, J. (1983). Composing and comprehending: Two sides of the same basic process. *Language Arts, 60*, 581-589.

4. Reading and writing develop together. (continued)

Sweet, A. (1993, November). *State of the art: Transforming ideas for teaching and learning to read.* Washington, DC: U.S. Department of Education, Office of Educational Research and Improvement.

Tierney, R. J., & Shannahan, T. (1991). Research on the reading-writing relationship: Interactions, transactions, and outcomes. In R. Barr, M. L. Kamil, P. Mosenthal, & P. D. Pearson (Eds.), *Handbook of reading research, 2.* New York, NY: Longman.

Wilde, S. (1992). *You kan red this! Spelling and punctuation for whole language classrooms, K-6.* Portsmouth, NH: Heinemann Educational Books.

5. Reading involves complex thinking.

Association for Supervision and Curriculum Development (ASCD) (1997). (How children learn: Theme issue). *Educational Leadership, 54(6).*

Caine, R. N., & Caine, G. (1991). *Making connections: Teaching and the human brain.* Alexandria, VA: Association for Supervision and Curriculum Development.

Caine, R. N., & Caine, G. (1997). *Education on the edge of possibility.* Alexandria, VA: Association for Supervision and Curriculum Development.

Commission on Student Learning. (1996, January). *Essential academic learning requirements: Reading, writing, communication, and mathematics.* Olympia, WA: Author.

International Reading Association & National Council of Teachers of English (1996). *Standards for the English language arts.* Newark, DE: International Reading Association & Urbana, IL: National Council of Teachers of English.

Palincsar, A. S., & Brown, A. (1984). Reciprocal teaching of comprehension-fostering and comprehension-monitoring activities. *Cognition and Instruction 2,* 117-175.

Rosenblatt, L. (1938/1976). *Literature as exploration.* New York, NY: Modern Language Association.

Rosenblatt, L. (1978). *The reader, the text, and the poem: The transactional theory of literary work.* Carbondale, IL: Southern Illinois University Press.

Ruddell, R., Ruddell, M., & Singer, H. (1994). *Theoretical models and processes of reading* (4th ed.). Newark, DE: International Reading Association.

Sweet, A. (1993, November). *State of the art: Transforming ideas for teaching and learning to read.* Washington, DC: U.S. Department of Education, Office of Educational Research and Improvement.

6. Environments rich in literacy experiences, resources, and models facilitate reading development.

Allington, R., & Cunningham, P. (1996). *Schools that work.* New York, NY: Harper Collins.

Bisset, D. (1969). *The amount and effect of recreational reading in selected fifth grade classes.* Unpublished doctoral dissertation, Syracuse University, New York, NY.

Bloome, D. (1991). Anthropology and research on teaching the English language arts. In J. Flood, J. Jensen, D. Lapp, & J. Squire (Eds.), *Handbook of Research on Teaching the English Language Arts.* New York, NY: Macmillan.

Cazden, C. B. (1986). Classroom discourse. In M. C. Wittrock (Ed.), *The handbook of research in teaching* (3rd ed.). New York, NY: Macmillan.

Chomsky, C. (1972). Stages in language development and reading exposure. *Harvard Educational Review, 42,* 1-33.

Cox, B., & Sulzby, E. (1984). Children's use of reference in told, dictated, and handwritten stories. *Research in the Teaching of English, 18,* 345-365.

Cullinan, B. (1987). *Children's literature in the reading program.* Newark, DE: International Reading Association.

Durkin, D. (1974-75). A six year study of children who learned to read in school at the age of four. *Reading Research Quarterly, 10,* 9-61.

Dyson, A. H. (1987). The value of "time off task": Young children's spontaneous talk and deliberate text. *Harvard Educational Review, 57,* 396-420.

Field, T. (1980). Preschool play: Effects of teacher/child ratios and organization of classroom space. *Child Study Journal, 10,* 191-205.

Froebel, F. (1974). *The education of man.* Clifton, NJ: Augustus M. Kelly.

Hoffman, J. V., Roser, N. L., & Farest, C. (1988). Literature sharing strategies in classrooms serving students from economically disadvantaged and language different home environments. In J. E. Readance & R. S. Baldwin (Eds.), *Dialogues in literacy research: Thirty-seventh yearbook of the National Reading Conference.* Chicago, IL: National Reading Conference.

Jett-Simpson, M. (1989). Creative drama and story comprehension. In J. W. Stewig & S. L. Sebesta (Eds.), *Using literature in the elementary classroom.* Urbana, IL: National Council of Teachers of English.

Johnson, D. W., & Johnson, R. T. (1987). *Learning together and alone: Cooperative, competitive, and individualistic learning* (2nd ed.) Englewood Cliffs, NJ: Prentice Hall.

6. Environments rich in literacy experiences, resources, and models facilitate reading development. (continued)

Krashen, S. (1995). *Every person a reader: An alternative to the California Task Force report on reading.* Culver City, CA: Language Education Associates.

Loughlin, C., & Martin, M. (1987). *Supporting literacy: Developing effective learning environments.* New York, NY: Teachers College Press.

Moore, G. (1986). Effects of spatial definition of behavior setting on children's behavior: A quasi-experimental field study. *Journal of Environmental Psychology, 6,* 205-231.

Morrow, L. M. (1988). Young children's responses to one-to-one story readings in school settings. *Reading Research Quarterly, 23,* 89-107.

Morrow, L. M. (1990). The impact of classroom environmental changes on the promotion of literacy during play. *Early Childhood Research Quarterly, 5,* 537-554.

Morrow, L. M. (1996). *Motivating reading and writing in diverse classrooms: Social and physical contexts in a literature-based program* (Research Report No. 28). Urbana, IL: National Council of Teachers of English.

Morrow, L. M., O'Connor, E. M., & Smith, J. (1990). Effects of a story reading program on the literacy development of at-risk kindergarten children. *Journal of Reading Behavior, 20*(2), 104-141.

Pappas, C., & Brown, E. (1987). Learning to read by reading: Learning how to extend the functional potential of language. *Research in the Teaching of English, 21,* 160-184.

Pearson, P. D. (1996). Foreword. In E. McIntyre & M. Pressley (Eds.), *Balanced instruction: Strategies and skills in whole language.* Norwood, MA: Christopher-Gordon Publishers.

Piaget, J., & Inhelder, B. (1969). *The psychology of the child.* New York, NY: Basic Books.

Rivlin, L., & Weinstein, C. S. (1984). Educational issues, school settings, and environmental psychology. *Journal of Environmental Psychology, 4,* 347-364.

Rusk, R., & Scotland, J. (1979). *Doctrines of the great educators.* New York, NY: St. Martin's Press.

Slavin, R.E. (1983). Non-cognitive outcomes. In J. M. Levine & M. C. Wang (Eds.), *Teacher and student perceptions: Implications for learning.* Hillsdale, NJ: Erlbaum.

Spivak, M. (1973). Archetypal place. *Architectural Forum, 40,* 40-44.

Sweet, A. (1993, November). *State of the art: Transforming ideas for teaching and learning to read.* Washington, DC: U.S. Department of Education, Office of Educational Research and Improvement.

6. Environments rich in literacy experiences, resources, and models facilitate reading development. (continued)

Taylor, D. (1983). *Family literacy: Young children learn to read and write.* Exeter, NH: Heinemann.

Teale, W. (1982). Toward a theory of how children learn to read and write naturally. *Language Arts, 59,* 555-570.

Teale, W. (1984). Reading to young children: Its significance for literacy development. In H. Goelman, A. Oberg, & F. Smith (Eds.), *Awakening to literacy.* Exeter, NH: Heinemann.

Teale, W. H., & Sulzby, E. (1987). Literacy acquisition in early childhood: The roles of access and mediation in storybook reading. In D. A. Wagner (Ed.), *The future of literacy in a changing world.* New York, NY: Pergamon Press.

Vygotsky, L. S. (1978). *Mind in society: The development of psychological processes.* Cambridge, MA: Harvard University Press.

7. Engagement in the reading task is key in successfully learning to read.

Brandt, D. (1990). *Literacy as involvement: The acts of writers, readers, and texts.* Carbondale, IL: Southern Illinois University Press.

Cambourne, B. (1988). *The whole story: Natural learning and the acquisition of literacy in the classroom.* Auckland, New Zealand: Ashton Scholastic.

Ford, M. (1992). *Motivating humans: Goals, emotions, and personal agency beliefs.* Newbury Park, CA: Sage Publications.

Gambrell, L., Almasi, J., Xie, Q., & Heland, V. (1995). Helping first graders get off to a running start in reading: A home-school-community program that enhances family literacy. In L. M. Morrow (Ed.), *Family literacy: Multiple perspectives to enhance literacy development.* Newark, DE: International Reading Association.

Gambrell, L., Palmer, B., & Coding, R. (1993). *Motivation to read.* Washington, DC: U.S. Department of Education, Office of Educational Research and Improvement.

Greenleaf, C. (1997). *The HERALD project, high school literacy task force: Action research agenda, 1995-1998.* San Francisco, CA: WestEd.

Guthrie, J. (1997, January). The director's corner. *NRRC News: A Newsletter of the National Reading Research Center,* p. 3.

McCombs, B. L. (1989). Self-regulated learning and academic achievement: A phenomenological view. In B. J. Zimmerman & D. H. Schunk (Eds.), *Self regulated learning and academic achievement: Theory, research, and practice.* New York, NY: Springer-Verlag.

7. Engagement in the reading task is key in successfully learning to read. (continued)

Maehr, M. (1976). Continuing motivation: An analysis of a seldom considered educational outcome. *Review of Educational Research, 46,* 443-462.

Morrow, L. M. (1992). The impact of a literature-based program on literacy achievement, use of literature, and attitudes of children from minority backgrounds. *Reading Research Quarterly, 27,* 250-275.

Morrow, L. M. (1996). Motivating reading and writing in diverse classrooms: Social and physical contexts in a literature-based program (Research Report No. 28). Urbana, IL: National Council of Teachers of English.

Morrow, L. M., & Weinstein, C. S. (1986). Encouraging voluntary reading: The impact of a literature program on children's use of library centers. *Reading Research Quarterly, 21,* 330-346.

National Academy of Education. (1991). *Research and the renewal of education.* New York, NY: Carnegie Corporation.

Oldfather, P. (1993). What students say about motivating experiences in a whole language classroom. *The Reading Teacher, 46,* 672-681.

Spaulding, C. I. (1992). The motivation to read and write. In J. W. Irwin & M. A. Doyle (Eds.), *Reading/writing connections: Learning from research.* Newark, DE: International Reading Association.

Wang, M. C., Haertel, G. D., & Walberg, H. J. (1990). What influences learning? A content analysis of review literature. *Journal of Educational Research, 84,* 30-43.

8. Children's understandings of print are not the same as adults' understandings.

Adams, M. J. (1990). *Beginning to read: Thinking and learning about print.* Cambridge, MA: The MIT Press.

Berdiansky, B., Cronnell, B., & Koehler, J. (1969). *Spelling sound relations and primary form-class descriptions for speech comprehension vocabularies of 6-9 year olds.* (Technical Report No. 15). Inglewood, CA: Southwest Regional Laboratory for Educational Research and Development.

Bruce, L. (1964). The analysis of word sounds by young children. *British Journal of Educational Psychology, 34,* 158-170.

Calfee, R. (1977). Assessment of individual reading skills: Basic research and practical applications. In A. S. Reber & D. L. Scarborough (Eds.), *Toward a psychology of reading.* New York, NY: Erlbaum.

Carbo, M. (1987). Reading style research: "What works" isn't always phonics. *Phi Delta Kappan, 68,* 431-435.

8. Children's understandings of print are not the same as adults' understandings.
(continued)

Clay, M. (1979). *Reading: The pattern of complex behavior*. Auckland, New Zealand: Heinemann.

Cunningham, P. (1995). *Phonics they use: Words for reading and writing* (2nd ed.). New York, NY: Harper Collins.

Ehri, L., & Wilce, L. (1980). The influence of orthography on readers' conceptualization of the phonemic structure of words. *Applied Psycholinguistics, 1*, 371-385.

Goodman, Y. (1986). Children coming to know literacy. In W. Teale & E. Sulzby (Eds.), *Emergent literacy: Reading and writing*. Norwood, NJ: Ablex.

Goswami, U. (1986). Children's use of analogy in learning to read: A developmental study. *Journal of Experimental Child Psychology, 42*, 73-83.

Goswami, U. (1988). Orthographic analogies and reading development. *The Quarterly Journal of Experimental Psychology, 40A*, 239-268.

Goswami, U., & Bryant, P. (1990). *Phonological skills and learning to read*. Hillsdale, NJ: Erlbaum.

Hanna, P. R., et al. (1966). *Phoneme-grapheme correspondences as cues to spelling improvement* (USOE Publication No. 32008). Washington, DC: Government Printing Office.

Liberman, I., Shankweiler, D., Fischer, F., & Carter, B. (1974). Explicit syllable and phoneme segmentation in the young child. *Journal of Experimental Child Psychology, 18*, 201-212.

Lie, A. (1991). Effects of a training program for stimulating skills in word analysis in first-grade children. *Reading Research Quarterly, 26*, 234-250.

Mann, V. (1986). Phonological awareness. *Cognition, 24*, 65-92.

Morias, J., Bertelson, P., Cary, L., & Alegria, J. (1986). Literacy training and speech segmentation. *Cognition, 24*, 45-64.

Moustafa, M. (1997). *Beyond traditional phonics: How children learn to read and how you can help them*. Portsmouth, NH: Heinemann.

Perfetti, C., Beck, I., Bell, L., & Hughes, C. (1987). Phonemic knowledge and learning to read are reciprocal: A longitudinal study of first grade children. *Merrill-Palmer Quarterly, 33*, 283-319.

Read, C., Yun-Fei, Z., Hong-Yin, N., & Bao-Gin, D. (1986). The ability to manipulate speech sounds depends on knowing alphabetic writing. *Cognition, 24*, 31-44.

8. Children's understandings of print are not the same as adults' understandings. (continued)

Rosner, J. (1974). Auditory analysis training with prereaders. *The Reading Teacher, 27*, 379-384.

Treiman, R. (1983). The structure of spoken syllables: Evidence from novel word games. Cognition, 15, 49-74.

Treiman, R. (1985). Onsets and rimes as units of spoken syllables: Evidence from children. *Journal of Experimental Psychology, 39*, 161-181.

Treiman, R. (1986). The division between onsets and rimes in English syllables. *Journal of Memory and Language, 25*, 476-491.

Treiman, R., & Baron, J. (1981). Segmental analysis ability: Development and relation to reading ability. In G. E. MacKinnon & T. G. Waller (Eds.), *Reading research: Advances in theory and practice* (Vol. 3). New York, NY: Academic Press.

Treiman, R., & Chafetz, J. (1987). Are there onset- and rime-like units in printed words? In M. Coltheart (Ed.), *Attention and performance XII: The psychology of reading*. Hillsdale, NJ: Erlbaum.

Tumner, W., & Nesdale, A. (1985). Phonemic segmentation and beginning reading. *Journal of Educational Psychology, 77*, 417-427.

Venezky, R. (1967). English orthography: Its graphical structure and its relation to sound. *Reading Research Quarterly, 2*, 75-106.

Venezky, R. (1970). Regularity in reading and spelling. In H. Levin & J. P. Williams (Eds.), *Basic studies on reading*. New York, NY: Basic.

Winner, H., Landerl, K., Linortner, R., & Hummer, P. (1991). The relationship of phonemic awareness to reading acquisition: More consequence than precondition but still important. *Cognition, 40*, 219-249.

Wylie, R., & Durrell, D. (1970). Teaching vowels through phonograms. *Elementary English, 47*, 787-791.

Yaden, D., & Templeton, S. (Eds.). (1986). *Metalinguistic awareness and beginning literacy: Conceptualizing what it means to read and write*. Portsmouth, NH: Heinemann Educational Books.

9. Children develop phonemic awareness and knowledge of phonics through a variety of literacy opportunities, models, and demonstrations.

Adams, M. (1990). *Beginning to read: Thinking and learning about print*. Cambridge, MA: The MIT Press.

9. Children develop phonemic awareness and knowledge of phonics through a variety of literacy opportunities, models, and demonstrations. (continued)

Allen, R. V. (1976). *Language experiences in communication*. Boston, MA: Allyn & Bacon.

Allington, R. L. (1997). Overselling phonics. *Reading Today, 15*(1), 15-16.

Anderson, R., Hiebert, E., Scott, J., & Wilkinson, I. (1985). *Becoming a nation of readers: The report on the commission on reading*. Champaign, IL: University of Illinois, Center for the Study of Reading.

Au, K. (1993). *Literacy instruction in multicultural settings*. New York, NY: Harcourt Brace.

Ball, E., & Blachman, B. A. (1991). Does phoneme awareness training in kindergarten make a difference in early word recognition and developmental spelling? *Reading Research Quarterly 26*(1), 49-66.

Beck, I., & Juel, C. (1995). The role of decoding in learning to read. *American Educator, 19*(2), 8, 21-25, 39-42.

Bond, G. L., & Dykstra, R. (1967). The cooperative research program in first grade reading instruction. *Reading Research Quarterly, 2*, 5-142.

Carnine, D., & Grossen, B. (1993). Phonics instruction comparing research and practice. *Teaching Exceptional Children, 25*(2), 22-25.

Chall, J. (1967/1983). *Learning to read: The great debate*. New York, NY: McGraw-Hill.

Chamot, A. (1993). Instructional practices enhance student achievement. *FORUM Newsletter of the National Clearinghouse for Bilingual Education, XVI*, 1, 4.

Chaney, C. (1992). Language development, metalinguistic skills, and print awareness in 3-year-old children. *Applied Psycholinguistics, 13*, 485-514.

Clarke, L. (1988). Invented versus traditional spelling in first graders' writings: Effects on learning to spell and read. *Research in the Teaching of English 22*, 281-309.

Clymer, T. (1963). The utility of phonic generalizations in the primary grades. *The Reading Teacher, 16*, 252-258.

Crawford, L. (1993). *Language and literacy in multicultural classrooms*. Needham Heights, MA: Allyn & Bacon.

Cummins, J. (1986). Empowering minority students: A framework for intervention. *Harvard Educational Review, 56*, 18-36.

Cunningham, A. E. (1990). Explicit versus implicit instruction in phonemic awareness. *Journal of Experimental Child Psychology, 50*, 429-444.

9. Children develop phonemic awareness and knowledge of phonics through a variety of literacy opportunities, models, and demonstrations. (continued)

Delpit, L. (1986). Skills and other dilemmas of a progressive Black educator. *Harvard Educational Review, 56,* 379-385.

Delpit, L. (1988). The silenced dialogue: Power and pedagogy in educating other people's children. *Harvard Educational Review, 58,* 280-298.

Foorman, B. (1995). Research on "The great debate": Code-oriented versus whole language approaches to reading instruction. *School Psychology Review, 24,* 376-392.

Foorman, B., Francis, D., Beeler, T., Winikates, D., & Fletcher, J. (Forthcoming). Early intervention for children with reading problems: Study designs and preliminary findings. *Learning Disabilities: A Multidisciplinary Journal.*

Fountas, I., & Pinnell, G. S. (1996). *Guided reading: Good first teaching for all children.* Portsmouth, NH: Heinemann Educational Books.

Freppon, P.A., & Dahl, K. L. (1991). Learning about phonics in a whole language classroom. *Language Arts, 68*(3), 190-197.

Gay, G. (1988). Designing relevant curricula for diverse learners. *Education and Urban Society, 20*(4), 327-340.

Goodman, K. (1965). A linguistic study of cues and miscues in reading. *Elementary English, 42,* 639-643.

Goswami, U. (1986). Children's use of analogy in learning to read: A developmental study. *Journal of Experimental Child Psychology, 42,* 73-83.

Goswami, U. (1988). Orthographic analogies and reading development. *The Quarterly Journal of Experimental Psychology, 40A,* 239-268.

Harste, J., Woodward, V., & Burke, C. (1984). *Language stories and literacy lessons.* Exeter, NH: Heinemann.

Hatcher, P., Hulme, C., & Ellis, A. (1994). Ameliorating early reading failure by integrating the teaching of reading and phonological skills: The phonological linkage hypothesis. *Child Development, 65,* 41-57.

Heath, S. B, Mangiola, L., Schecter, R., & Hall, G. (Eds.). (1991). *Children of promise: Literate activity in linguistically and culturally diverse classrooms.* Washington, DC: National Education Association.

House, E., Glass, G., McLean, L., & Walker, D. (1978). No simple answer: Critique of the follow through evaluation. *Harvard Educational Review, 48,* 128-160.

9. Children develop phonemic awareness and knowledge of phonics through a variety of literacy opportunities, models, and demonstrations. (continued)

International Reading Association. (1997a). IRA takes stand on phonics. *Reading Today 14*(5), p. 1.

International Reading Association. (1997b). *The role of phonics in reading instruction.* (A position statement of the International Reading Association, January, 1997). Newark, DE: International Reading Association.

Juel, C. (1988). Learning to read and write: A longitudinal study of 54 children from first through fourth grades. *Journal of Educational Psychology, 78,* 243-255.

Juel, C. (1991). Beginning reading. In R. Barr, M. L. Kamil, P. Mosenthal, & P. D. Pearson (Eds.), *Handbook of reading research, 2.* New York, NY: Longman.

Juel, C. (1994). *Learning to read and write in one elementary school.* New York, NY: Springer-Verlag.

Kasten, W., & Clarke, B. (1989). *Reading/writing readiness for preschool and kindergarten children: A whole language approach.* Sanibel, FL: Florida Educational Research Development Council, Inc. (FERC) Research Project Report (ERIC Document Reproduction Service No. 312 041)

Knapp, M., & Shields, P. (1990). Reconceiving academic instruction for the children of poverty. *Phi Delta Kappan, 71,* 753-758.

Kucer, S. (1985). Predictability and readability: The same rose with different names? In M. Douglass (Ed.), *Claremont Reading Conference 49th Yearbook.* Claremont, CA: Claremont Graduate School.

Lundberg, I., Frost, J., & Petersen, O. (1988). Effects of an extensive program for stimulating phonological awareness in preschool children. *Reading Research Quarterly, 23,* 263-284.

Mann, V. (1986). Phonological awareness: The role of reading experience. *Cognition, 24,* 65-92.

Moustafa, M. (1995). Children's productive phonological recoding. *Reading Research Quarterly, 30,* 464-476.

Moustafa, M. (1997). *Beyond traditional phonics: How children learn to read and how you can help them.* Portsmouth, NH: Heinemann.

Morias, J., Bertelson, P., Cary, L., & Alegria, J. (1986). Literacy training and speech segmentation. *Cognition, 24,* 45-64.

Nicholson, T. (1991). Do children read words better in context or in lists? A classic study revisited. *Journal of Educational Psychology, 83,* 444-450.

9. Children develop phonemic awareness and knowledge of phonics through a variety of literacy opportunities, models, and demonstrations. (continued)

O'Donnell, M., & Wood, M. (1992). *Becoming a reader: A developmental approach to reading instruction.* Boston, MA: Allyn & Bacon.

Ovando, C. (1993). Language diversity and education. In J. Banks & C. McGhee Banks (Eds.), *Multicultural education: Issues and perspectives.* Boston, MA: Allyn & Bacon.

Pearson, P. D. (1993). Focus on research. Teaching and learning reading: A research perspective. *Language Arts, 70,* 502-511.

Pogrow, S. (1992, April). What to do about Chapter 1: An alternative view from the street. *Phi Delta Kappan,* 624-630.

Purcell-Gates, V., McIntyre, E. & Freppon, P. (1995). Learning written storybook language in school: A comparison of low-SES children in skills-based and whole language classrooms. *American Educational Research Journal, 32*(3), 659-685.

Read, C. (1975). *Children's categorizations of speech sounds in English* (Research Report No. 17). Urbana, IL: National Council of Teachers of English.

Read, C. (1986). *Children's creative spelling.* New York: Routledge.

Ribowsky, H. (1985). The effects of a code emphasis approach and a whole language approach upon emergent literacy of kindergarten children. (Report No. CS-008-397). New York, NY: Available from ERIC Document Reproduction Service. (ERIC Document Reproduction Service No. ED 269 720)

Rhodes, L. (1979). Comprehension and predictability: An analysis of beginning reading materials. In J. Harste & R. Carey (Eds.), *New perspectives on comprehension.* Bloomington, IN: Indiana University, School of Education.

Schweinhart, L., Weikart, D., & Larner, M. (1986). Consequences of three preschool curriculum models through age 15. *Early Childhood Research Quarterly,* 1, 15-45.

Schickedanz, J. (1986). *More than ABC's: The early stages of reading and writing.* Washington, DC: National Association for the Education of Young Children.

Shannon, P. (1996). Mad as hell. *Language Arts, 73*(1), 14-19.

Stahl, S. A., McKenna, M. C., & Pangucco, J. R. (1994). The effects of whole language instruction: An update and a reappraisal. *Educational Psychologist, 29,* 175-185.

Stanovich, K. (1986). Matthew effects in reading: Some consequences of individual differences in the acquisition of literacy. *Reading Research Quarterly, 21,* 360-407.

9. Children develop phonemic awareness and knowledge of phonics through a variety of literacy opportunities, models, and demonstrations. (continued)

Stanovich, K. (1991). Word recognition: Changing perspectives. In R. Barr, M. Kamil, P. Mosenthal, & P. D. Pearson (Eds.), *Handbook of reading research, 2*. New York, NY: Macmillan.

Stebbins, L., St. Pierre, R., Proper, E., Anderson, R., & Cerva, T. (1977). *Education as experimentation: A planned variation model, An evaluation of follow through* (Vol. IV-A). Cambridge, MA: ABT Associates.

Stice, C., & Bertrand, N. (1990). *Whole language and the emergent literacy of at-risk children: A 2-year comparative study*. Nashville, TN: Tennessee State University Center for Excellence.

Sweet, A. (1993, November). *State of the art: Transforming ideas for teaching and learning to read*. Washington, DC: U.S. Department of Education, Office of Educational Research and Improvement.

Tharp, R. (1989). Psychocultural variables and constants: Effects on teaching and learning in schools. *American Psychologist, 44*, 349-359.

Thompson, R., Mixon, G., & Serpell, R. (1996). Engaging minority students in reading: Focus on the urban learner. In L. Baker, P. Afflerbach, & D. Reinking (Eds.), *Developing engaged readers in school and home communities*. Hillsdale, NJ: Erlbaum.

Tumner, W., Herriman, M., & Nesdale, A. (1988). Metalinguistic abilities and beginning reading. *Reading Research Quarterly, 23*, 134-158.

Weaver, C. (1994). *Reading process and practice: From socio-psycholinguistics to whole language*. Portsmouth, NH: Heinemann.

Weaver, C., Gillmeister-Krause, L., & Vento-Zogby, G. (1996). *Creating support for effective literacy education: Workshop materials and handouts*. Portsmouth, NH: Heinemann.

Wilde, S. (1992). *You kan red this! Spelling and punctuation for whole language classrooms, K-6*. Portsmouth, NH: Heinemann Educational Books.

Winner, H., Landerl, K., Linortner, R., & Hummer, P. (1991). The relationship of phonemic awareness to reading acquisition: More consequence than precondition but still important. *Cognition, 40*, 219-249.

Winsor, P., & Pearson, P. D. (1992). *Children at-risk: Their phonemic awareness development in holistic instruction* (Technical Report No. 556). Urbana, IL: University of Illinois, Center for the Study of Reading.

10. Children learn successful reading strategies in the context of real reading.

Baumann, J. (1984). The effectiveness of a direct instruction paradigm for teaching main idea comprehension. *Reading Research Quarterly, 20*(1), 93-115.

Beck, I., Omanson, R., & McKeown, M. (1982). An instructional redesign of reading lessons: Effects on comprehension. *Reading Research Quarterly, 17*(4), 462-481.

Brown, H., & Cambourne, B. (1990). *Read and retell.* Portsmouth, NH: Heinemann Educational Books.

Clay, M. (1972). *The early detection of reading difficulties: A diagnostic survey with recovery procedures.* Exeter, NH: Heinemann.

Cooper, J. D. (1993). *Literacy: Helping children construct meaning.* Boston, MA: Houghton Mifflin Company.

Englert, C., & Hiebert, E. (1984). Children's developing awareness of text structures in expository materials. *Journal of Educational Psychology, 76,* 65-74.

Goodman, K. (1965). A linguistic study of cues and miscues in reading. *Elementary English, 42,* 639-643.

Goodman, Y., Watson, D., & Burke, C. (1987). *Reading miscue inventory.* Katonah, NY: Richard C. Owen.

McGee, L. (1982). Awareness of text structure: Effects on children's recall of expository text. *Reading Research Quarterly, 17,* 581-590.

Myer, B., Brandt, D., & Bluth, G. (1980). Use of top-level structure in text: Key for reading comprehension of ninth-grade students. *Reading Research Quarterly, 16,* 73-103.

Palincsar, A., & Brown, A. (1984). Reciprocal teaching of comprehension-fostering and comprehension-monitoring activities. *Cognition and Instruction, 2,* 117-175.

Paris, S., Lipson, M., & Wixon, K. (1983). Becoming a strategic reader. *Contemporary Educational Psychology, 8,* 293-316.

Paris, S., Wasik, B., & Turner, J. (1991). The development of strategic readers. In R. Barr, M. Kamil, P. Mosenthal, & P.D. Pearson (Eds.), *Handbook of reading research, 2.* New York, NY: Macmillan.

Pearson, P. D. (1993). Focus on research. Teaching and learning reading: A research perspective. *Language Arts, 70,* 502-511.

Pressley, M., El-Dinary, P., Gaskins, I., Schuder, T., Bergman, J., Almasi, J., & Brown, R. (1992). Beyond direct explanation: Transactional instruction of reading comprehension instruction. *The Elementary School Journal, 92*(5), 513-555.

10. Children learn successful reading strategies in the context of real reading.
(continued)

Pressley, M., Gaskins, I., Wile, D., Cunicelli, E., & Sheridan, J. (1991). Teaching strategy across the curriculum: A case study at Benchmark School. In S. McCormick & J. Zutell (Eds.), *40th yearbook of the National Reading Conference*. Chicago, IL: National Reading Conference.

Pressley, M., Schuder, T., & Bergman, J. (1992). A researcher-educator collaborative interview study of transactional comprehension strategies instruction. *Journal of Educational Psychology, 84*, 231-46.

Rinehart, S., Stahl, S., & Erickson, L. (1986). Some effects of summarization training on reading and studying. *Reading Research Quarterly, 21*, 422-438.

Sweet, A. (1993, November). *State of the art: Transforming ideas for teaching and learning to read*. Washington, DC: U.S. Department of Education, Office of Educational Research and Improvement.

Taylor, B. (1980). Children's memory for expository text after reading. *Reading Research Quarterly, 15*, 399-411.

11. Children learn best when teachers employ a variety of strategies to model and demonstrate reading knowledge, strategy, and skills.

Adams, M. (1990). *Beginning to read: Thinking and learning about print*. Cambridge, MA: The MIT Press.

Allington, R. (1980). Poor readers don't get to read much in reading groups. *Language Arts, 57*(8), 873-875.

Almasi, J. (1995). The nature of fourth graders' sociocognitive conflicts in peer-led and teacher-led discussions of literature. *Reading Research Quarterly, 30*(3), 314-351.

Anderson, R., Wilson, P., & Fielding, L. (1988). Growth in reading and how children spend their time outside of school. *Reading Research Quarterly, 23*(3), 285-303.

Applebee, A., & Langer, J. (1983). Instructional scaffolding: Reading and writing as natural activities. *Language Arts, 60*, 168-175.

Au, K. (1991, April). A special issue on organizing for instruction. *The Reading Teacher, 44*, 534.

Au, K. (1993). *Literacy instruction in multicultural settings*. New York, NY: Harcourt Brace.

Barr, R. (1989). The social organization of literacy instruction. In *Cognitive and social perspectives for literacy research and instruction: The thirty-eighth yearbook of the National Reading Conference*. Chicago, IL: The National Reading Conference.

11. Children learn best when teachers employ a variety of strategies to model and demonstrate reading knowledge, strategy, and skills. (continued)

Brown, A., & Palincsar, A. (1989). Guided, cooperative learning and individual knowledge acquisition. In L. Resnick (Ed.), *Knowing, learning, and instruction: Essays in honor of Robert Glaser*. Hillsdale, NJ: Erlbaum.

Bruner, J. (1975). The ontogenesis of speech acts. *Journal of Child Language, 3*, 1-19.

Caine, N., & Caine, M. (1997). *Education on the edge of possibility*. Alexandria, VA: Association for Supervision and Curriculum Development.

Cambourne, B., & Rousch, P. (1982). How do learning disabled children read? *Topics in Learning and Learning Disabilities, 1*, 59-68.

Clark, M. (1976). *Young fluent readers: What can they teach us?* London, United Kingdom: Heinemann.

Clay, M. (1991a). *Becoming literate: The construction of inner control*. Portsmouth, NH: Heinemann Educational Books.

Clay, M. (1991b). Introducing a new storybook to young readers. *The Reading Teacher, 45*, 264-73.

Cochran-Smith, M. (1984). *The making of a reader*. Norwood, NJ: Ablex.

Cohen, D. (1968). The effects of literature on vocabulary and reading achievement. *Elementary English, 45*, 209-13, 217.

Cunningham, P., Hall, D., & Defee, M. (1991). Non-ability grouped, multilevel instruction: A year in a first grade classroom. *The Reading Teacher, 44*, 566-571.

Davidson, J. (1985). What you think is going on, isn't: Eighth grade students' introspections of discussions in science and social studies lessons. In J. A. Niles & R. Lalik (Eds.), *Issues in literacy: A research perspective*. Rochester, NY: National Reading Conference.

Doise, W., & Mugney, G. (1984). *The social development of the intellect*. Oxford, United Kongdom: Pergamon Press.

Durkin, D. (1966). *Children who read early*. New York, NY: Teachers College Press.

Eeds, M., & Wells, D. (1989). Grand conversations: An exploration of meaning construction in literature study groups. *Research in the Teaching of English, 23*, 4-29.

Flood, J., Lapp, D., Flood, S., & Nagel, G. (1992). Am I allowed to group? Using flexible patterns for effective instruction. *The Reading Teacher, 45*(8), 608-616.

11. Children learn best when teachers employ a variety of strategies to model and demonstrate reading knowledge, strategy, and skills. (continued)

Fountas, I., & Pinnell, G. S. (1996). *Guided reading: Good first teaching for all children.* Portsmouth, NH: Heinemann Educational Books.

Gambrell, L. (1996). What research reveals about discussion. In J. Almasi & L. Gambrell (Eds.), *Lively Discussions! Fostering Engaged Reading.* Newark, DE: International Reading Association.

Gersten, R., & Carnine, D. (1986). Direct instruction in reading comprehension. *Educational Leadership, 43,* 70-78.

Goatley, V., & Raphael, T. (1992). Non-traditional learners' written and dialogic response to literature. In C. Kinzer & D. Leu (Eds.), *Literacy research, theory, and practice: Views from many perspectives.* Chicago, IL: National Reading Conference.

Goodman, Y. (1984). The development of initial literacy. In H. Goelman, A. Oberg, & F. Smith (Eds.), *Awakening to literacy.* Exeter, NH: Heinemann.

Goodman, Y., Watson, D., & Burke, C. (1987). *Reading miscue inventory.* Katonah, NY: Richard C. Owen.

Green, J., & Harker, J. (1982). Reading to children: A communicative process. In J. Langer & M. Smith-Burke (Eds.), *Reader meets author/Bridging the gap: A psycholinguistic and sociolinguistic perspective.* Newark, DE: International Reading Association.

Green, J., & Wallet, C. (1981). Mapping instructional conversations: A sociolinguistic ethnography. In J. Green & C. Wallet (Eds.), *Ethnography and language in educational settings.* Norwood, NJ: Ablex.

Guthrie, J., Schafer, W., Wang, Y., & Afflerbach, P. (1995). Influences of instruction on reading engagement: An empirical exploration of a social-cognitive framework of reading activity. *Reading Research Quarterly, 30*(1), 8-25.

Harste, J., & Burke, C. (1980). Understanding the hypothesis: It's the teacher that makes the difference. In B. Farr & D. Strickler (Eds.), *Reading comprehension: Resource guide.* Bloomington, IN: Indiana University Reading Programs.

Heath, S. B. (1983). *Ways with words.* Cambridge, United Kingdom: Cambridge University Press.

Hiebert, E. (1983). An examination of ability grouping for reading instruction. *Reading Research Quarterly, 18,* 231-55.

Hoffman, J. (1981). Is there a legitimate place for oral reading instruction in a developmental reading program? *Elementary School Journal, 81,* 305-310.

Holdaway, D. (1979). *The foundations of literacy.* Sydney, Australia: Ashton Scholastic.

11. Children learn best when teachers employ a variety of strategies to model and demonstrate reading knowledge, strategy, and skills. (continued)

Horowitz, R., & Freeman, S. (1995). Robots vs. spaceships: The role of discussion in kindergartners' and second graders' preferences for science texts. *The Reading Teacher, 49,* 30-40.

Hudgins, B., & Edelman, S. (1986). Teaching critical thinking skills to fourth and fifth graders through teacher-led small-group discussions. *Journal of Educational Research, 79,* 333-342.

Indrisano, R., & Parratore, J. (1991). Classroom contexts for literacy learning. In J. Flood, J. Jensen, D. Lapp, & J. Squire (Eds.), *Handbook of research on teaching the English language arts.* New York, NY: Macmillan.

Johnson, D., & Johnson, R. (1979). Conflict in the classroom: Controversy and learning. *Review of Educational Research, 49,* 51-70.

Langer, J. (1986). Reading, writing, and understanding: An analysis of the construction of meaning. *Written Communication, 3*(2), 219-267.

Langer, J. (1991). Discussion as exploration: Literature and the horizon of possibilities. In G. Newell & R. Durst (Eds.), *The role of discussion and writing in the teaching and learning of literature.* Norwood, MA: Christopher Gordon Publishers.

Leal, D. (1992). The nature of talk about three types of text during peer group discussions. *Journal of Reading Behavior, 24*(3), 313-338.

Lyons, C., Pinnell, G. S., & Deford, D. (1993). *Partners in learning: Teachers and children in reading recovery.* New York, NY: Teachers College Press.

Martinez, M., & Roser, N. (1985). Read it again: The value of repeated readings during storytime. *The Reading Teacher, 38,* 782-786.

McGee, L. (1992). An exploration of meaning construction in first graders' grand conversations. In C. Kinzer & D. Leu (Eds.), *Literacy research, theory, and practice: Views from many perspectives* [41st Yearbook of the National Reading Conference]. Chicago, IL: National Reading Conference.

McKenzie, M. (1986). *Journeys into literacy.* Huddersfield, United Kingdom: Schofield & Sims.

Meek, M. (1988). *How texts teach what readers learn.* Stoud, United Kingdom: The Thimble Press.

Morrow, L. M., & Smith, J. (1990). The effects of group size on interactive storybook reading. *Reading Research Quarterly, 25,* 213-231.

11. Children learn best when teachers employ a variety of strategies to model and demonstrate reading knowledge, strategy, and skills. (continued)

Morrow, L. M., & Weinstein, C. S. (1986). Encouraging voluntary reading: The impact of a literature program on children's use of library centers. *Reading Research Quarterly, 21*, 330-346.

Mugney, G., & Doise, W. (1978). Socio-cognitive conflict and structure of individual and collective performances. *European Journal of Social Psychology, 8*, 181-192.

Ninio, A. (1980). Picture book reading in mother-infant dyads belonging to two subgroups in Israel. *Child Development, 51*, 587-590.

O'Flavahan, J., Stein, S., Wiencek, J., & Marks, T. (1992). *Interpretive development in peer discussionabout literature: An exploration of the teacher's role* [Final report to the trustees of the National Council of Teachers of English]. Urbana, IL: National Council of Teachers of English

Palincsar, A. (1987, January). Reciprocal teaching: Can student discussions boost comprehension? *Instructor*, 56-60.

Palincsar, A., & Brown, A. (1984). Reciprocal teaching of comprehension-fostering and comprehension-monitoring activities. *Cognition and Instruction, 2*, 117-175.

Palincsar, A., Brown, A., & Martin, S. (1987). Peer interaction in reading comprehension instruction. *Educational Psychologist, 22*, 231-253.

Pappas, C., & Brown, E. (1987). Learning to read by reading: Learning how to extend the functional potential of language. *Research in the Teaching of English, 21*, 160-184.

Pearson, P. D. (1996). Foreword. In E. McIntyre & M. Pressley (Eds.), *Balanced instruction: Strategies and skills in whole language*. Norwood, MA: Christopher-Gordon Publishers.

Pflaum, S., & Bryan, T. (1982). Oral reading research and learning disabled children. *Topics in Learning and Learning Disabilities, 1*, 33-42.

Philips, S. (1973). Participant structures and communicative competence: Warm Springs children in community and classroom. In C. Cazden, V. John, & D. Hymes (Eds.), *Functions of language in the classroom*. New York, NY: Teachers College Press.

Pinnell, G. S., Pikulski, J., Wixson, K., Campbell, J., Gough, P., & Beatty, A. (1995). *Listening to children read aloud: Data from NAEP's integrated reading performance record at grade 4*. Washington, DC: National Center for Education Statistics.

Poplin, M. (1988). Holistic/constructivist principles of the teaching/learning process: Implications for the field of learning disabilities. *Journal of Learning Disabilities, 21*, 401-416.

11. Children learn best when teachers employ a variety of strategies to model and demonstrate reading knowledge, strategy, and skills. (continued)

Prawat, R. (1989). Promoting access to knowledge, strategy, and disposition in students: A research synthesis. *Review of Educational Research, 59*(1), 1-41.

Raphael, T. (1986). Teaching question answer relationships, revisited. *The Reading Teacher, 39*, 516-522.

Raphael, T., & McMahon, S. (1994). Book club: An alternative framework for reading instruction. *The Reading Teacher, 48*(2), 102-116.

Rhodes, L., & Dudley-Marling, C. (1996). *Readers and writers with a difference: A holistic approach to teaching struggling readers and writers* (2nd ed.). Portsmouth, NH: Heinemann Educational Books.

Roehler, L., & Duffy, G. (1991). Teachers' instructional actions. In R. Barr, M. Kamil, P. Mosenthal, & P. D. Pearson (Eds.), *Handbook of reading research, 2*. New York, NY: Macmillan.

Rogers, T. (1991). Students as literary critics: The interpretive experiences, beliefs, and processes of ninth-grade students. *Journal of Reading Behavior, 23*, 391-423.

Routman, R. (1991). *Invitations: Changing as teachers and learners K-12*. Portsmouth, NH: Heinemann Educational Books.

Rowe, D. (1987). Literacy learning as an intertextual process. *National Reading Conference Yearbook, 36*, 101-112.

Samuels, S. (1994). Toward a theory of automatic information processing in reading, revisited. In R. Ruddell, M. Ruddell, & H. Singer (Eds.), *Theoretical models and processes of reading*. Newark, DE: International Reading Association.

Schickedanz, J. (1978). Please read that story again! Exploring relationships between story reading and learning to read. *Young Children, 33*, 48-55.

Shannon, P. (1985). Reading instruction and social class. *Language Arts, 62*, 604-613.

Short, K., Harste, J., & Burke, C. (1996). *Creating classrooms for authors and inquirers*. Portsmouth, NH: Heinemann Educational Books.

Slavin, R. (1990). *Cooperative learning: Theory, research, and practice*. Englewood Cliffs, NJ: Prentice-Hall.

Snow, C. (1983). Literacy and language: Relationships during the preschool years. *Harvard Educational Review, 53*(2), 165-189.

11. Children learn best when teachers employ a variety of strategies to model and demonstrate reading knowledge, strategy, and skills. (continued)

Strickland, D., & Ascher, C. (1992). Low-income African American children and public schooling. In P. Jackson (Ed.), *Handbook of research on curriculum*. New York, NY: Macmillan.

Sulzby, E. (1985). Children's emergent reading favorite storybooks. *Reading Research Quarterly, 20*, 458-481.

Sweigert, W. (1991). Classroom talk, knowledge development, and writing. *Research in the Teaching of English, 25*, 469-496.

Taubenheim, B., & Christensen, J. (1978). Let's shoot "Cock Robin"! Alternatives to round robin reading. *Language Arts, 55*, 975-977.

Taylor, D. (1983). Family literacy: *Young children learn to read and write*. Exeter, NH: Heinemann.

Taylor, N., & Connor, O. (1982). Silent vs. oral reading: The rational instructional use of both processes. *The Reading Teacher, 35*, 440-443.

Teale, W., & Sulzby, E. (Eds.). (1986). *Emergent literacy: Reading and writing*. Norwood, NJ: Ablex.

Thompson, R., Mixon, G., & Serpell, R. (1996). Engaging minority students in reading: Focus on the urban learner. In L. Baker, P. Afflerbach, & D. Reinking (Eds.), *Developing engaged readers in school and home communities*. Hillsdale, NJ: Erlbaum.

True, J. (1979). Round robin reading is for the birds. *Language Arts, 56*, 918-921.

Villaume, S., & Hopkins, L. (1995). A transactional and sociocultural view of response in a fourth-grade literature discussion group. *Reading Research and Instruction, 34*, 190-203.

Watkins, M., & Edwards, V. (1992). Extracurricular reading and reading achievement: The rich stay rich and the poor don't read. *Reading Improvement, 29*(4), 236-242.

Wells, G. (1986). *The meaning makers*. Portsmouth, NH: Heinemann.

White, J. (1990). Involving different social and cultural groups in discussion. In W. Wilen (Ed.), Teaching and learning through discussion. Springfield, IL: Charles C. Thomas.

Wiencek, J., & O'Flavahan, J. (1994). From teacher-led to peer discussions about literature: Suggestions for making the shift. *Language Arts, 71*, 488-498.

Winklejohann, R., & Gallant, R. (1979). Queries: Why oral reading? *Language Arts, 56*, 950-953.

11. Children learn best when teachers employ a variety of strategies to model and demonstrate reading knowledge, strategy, and skills. (continued)

Wong Fillmore, L., & Meyer, L. (1992). The curriculum and linguistic minorities. In P. Jackson (Ed.), *Handbook of research on curriculum.* New York, NY: Macmillan.

Wong, S., Groth, L., & O'Flavahan, J. (1994). *Characterizing teacher-student interaction in Reading Recovery lessons* [National Reading Research Center Report No. 17, National Reading Research Project of the Universities of Georgia and Maryland]. Athens, GA: University of Georgia.

12. Children need the opportunity to read, read, read.

Allington, R. (1977). If they don't read much, how they ever gonna get good? *Journal of Reading, 21,* 57-61.

Allington, R. (1980). Poor readers don't get to read much in reading groups. *Language Arts, 57*(8), 873-875.

Allington, R., & Cunningham, P. (1996). *Schools that work.* New York, NY: Harper Collins.

Anderson, R., Wilson, P., & Fielding, L. (1988). Growth in reading and how children spend their time outside of school. *Reading Research Quarterly, 23,* 285-303.

Elley, W., & Mangubhai, F. (1983). The impact of reading on second language learning. *Reading Research Quarterly, 19,* 53-67.

Fractor, J., Woodruff, M., Martinez, M., & Teale, W. (1993). Let's not miss opportunities to promote voluntary reading: Classroom libraries in the elementary school. *The Reading Teacher, 46,* 476-484.

Guice, S., & Allington, R. (1994). It's more than reading real books: 10 ways to enhance the implications of literature-based instruction. Albany, NY: National Research Center on Literature Teaching and Learning.

Guthrie, J., & Greaney, V. (1991). Literacy acts. In R. Barr, M. Kamil, P. Mosenthal, & P. D. Pearson (Eds.), *Handbook of reading research, 2.* New York, NY: Macmillan.

Herman, P., Anderson, R., Pearson, P. D., & Nagy, W. (1987). Incidental acquisition of word meaning from expositions with varied text features. *Reading Research Quarterly, 22,* 263-284.

Holdaway, D. (1979). *The foundations of literacy.* Sydney, Australia: Ashton Scholastic.

Ingham, J. (1982). *Books and reading development: The Bradford book flood experiment* (2nd ed.). Exeter, NH: Heinemann Educational Books.

Irving, A. (1980). Promoting voluntary reading for children and young people. Paris, France: Unesco.

12. Children need the opportunity to read, read, read. (continued)

Krashen, S. (1993). *The power of reading.* Englewood, CO: Libraries Unlimited.

Krashen, S. (1995). *Every person a reader: An alternative to the California Task Force report on reading.* Culver City, CA: Language Education Associates.

Lamme, L. (1976). Are reading habits and abilities related? *The Reading Teacher, 30,* 21-27.

Pearson, P. D. (1993). Focus on research. Teaching and learning reading: A research perspective. *Language Arts, 70,* 502-511.

Pearson, P. D., & Fielding, L. (1991). Comprehension instruction. In R. Barr, M. Kamil, P. Mosenthal, & P. D. Pearson (Eds.), *Handbook of reading research, 2.* New York, NY: Macmillan.

Pinnell, G. (1989). Success for at-risk children in a program that combines reading and writing. In J. Mason (Ed.), *Reading and writing connections.* Boston, MA: Allyn & Bacon.

Speigel, D. (1981). *Reading for pleasure: Guidelines.* Newark, DE: International Reading Association.

Stanovich, K. (1986). Matthew effects in reading: Some consequences of individual differences in the acquisition of literacy. *Reading Research Quarterly, 21,* 360-407.

13. Monitoring the development of reading processes is vital to student success.

Allington, R., & Walmsley, S. (Eds.). (1995). *No quick fix: Rethinking literacy programs in America's elementary schools.* Newark, DE: International Reading Association.

Brown, H., & Cambourne, B. (1990). *Read and retell.* Portsmouth, NH: Heinemann Educational Books.

Brown, C., & Lytle, S. (1988). Merging assessment and instruction: Protocols in the classroom. In S. Glazer, L. Searfoss, & L. Gentile (Eds.), *Reexamining reading diagnosis: New trends and procedures.* Newark, DE: International Reading Association.

Clay, M. (1972). *The early detection of reading difficulties: A diagnostic survey with recovery procedures.* Exeter, NH: Heinemann.

Clay, M. (1991). *Becoming literate: The construction of inner control.* Portsmouth, NH: Heinemann Educational Books.

Clay, M. (1993). *An observation survey of early literacy achievement.* Portsmouth, NH: Heinemann Educational Books.

13. Monitoring the development of reading processes is vital to student success.
(continued)

Cochrane, O., Cochrane, D., Scalena, S., & Buchanan, E. (1984). *Reading, writing, and caring*. Winnipeg, Manitoba, Canada: Whole Language Consultants. (Distributed by Richard C. Owen).

Commission on Student Learning. (1996, January). *Essential academic learning requirements: Reading, writing, communication, and mathematics*. Olympia, WA: Author.

Darling-Hammond, L. (1991). The implications of testing policy for quality and equality. *Phi Delta Kappan, 73*, 220-225.

Goodman, Y., Watson, D., & Burke, C. (1987). *Reading miscue inventory*. Katonah, NY: Richard C. Owen.

Holdaway, D. (1979). *The foundations of literacy*. Sydney, Australia: Ashton Scholastic.

International Reading Association & National Council of Teachers of English. (1996). *Standards for the English language arts*. Newark, DE: International Reading Association & Urbana, IL: National Council of Teachers of English.

Leslie, L., & Caldwell, J. (1990). *Qualitative Reading Inventory*. New York, NY: Harper Collins.

Mullis, I., Campbell, J., & Farstrup, A. (1992). *Executive summary of the NAEP 1992 reading report card for the nation and the states: Data from the national and trial state assessments*. Washington, DC: National Center for the Education Statistics.

Pinnell, G. S., Pikulski, J., Wixson, K., Campbell, J., Gough, P., & Beatty, A.. (1995). *Listening to children read aloud: Data from NAEP's integrated reading performance record at grade 4*. Washington, DC: National Center for Education Statistics.

Rhodes, L. (1993). *Literacy assessment: Handbook of forms*. Portsmouth, NH: Heinemann Educational Books.

Rhodes, L., & Dudley-Marling, C. (1996). *Readers and writers with a difference: A holistic approach to teaching struggling readers and writers* (2nd ed.). Portsmouth, NH: Heinemann Educational Books.

Ruddell, R., & Ruddell, M. (1994). Language acquisition and literacy processes. In R. Ruddell, M. Ruddell, & H. Singer (Eds.), *Theoretical models and processes of reading*. Newark, DE: International Reading Association.

Stallman, A., & Pearson, P. D. (1990). Formal measures of early literacy. In L. M. Morrow & J. Smith (Eds.), *Assessment for instruction in early literacy*. Englewood Cliffs, NJ: Prentice-Hall.

13. Monitoring the development of reading processes is vital to student success. (continued)

Williams, P., Reese, C., Campbell, J., Mazzeo, J., & Phillips, G. (1995, October). *NAEP 1994 reading: A first look* [Findings from the National Assessment of Educational Progress]. Washington, DC: National Center for Education Statistics.

Conclusion

Allington, R., & Cunningham, P. (1996). *Schools that work: Where all children read and write.* New York, NY: Harper Collins.

Allington, R., & McGill-Franzen, A. (1997, May). *Improving schools' responses to children on the edge.* Paper presented at the International Reading Association Annual Convention, Atlanta, GA.

Baumann, J. (1997, May). *Reflections on teaching struggling readers across grade levels.* Paper presented at the International Reading Association Annual Convention, Atlanta, GA.

Brown, H., & Cambourne, B. (1990). *Read and retell.* Portsmouth, NH: Heinemann Educational Books.

Carnegie Corporation of New York. (1996, September). *Years of promise: A comprehensive learning strategy for America's children* [The report of the Carnegie Task Force on Learning in the Primary Grades]. New York, NY: Author.

Clay, M. M. (1991). *Becoming literate: The construction of inner control.* Portsmouth, NH: Heineman.

Dreher, M. J., & Slater, W. H. (1992). Elementary school literacy: Critical issues. In M. J. Dreher & W. H. Slater (Eds.). *Elementary school literacy: Critical issues* (pp. 3-25). Norwood, MA: Christopher-Gordon Publishers, Inc.

Flippo, R. (1997, May). *Reaching consensus in literacy education: Beginnings of professional and political unity.* Symposium conducted at the International Reading Association Annual Convention, Atlanta, GA.

Guthrie, J., Schafer, W., Wang, Y., & Afflerbach, P. (1995). Influences of instruction on reading engagement: An empirical exploration of a social-cognitive framework of reading activity. *Reading Research Quarterly, 30*(1), 8-25.

Harste, J. C., Burke, C. L. & Woodward, V. A. (1983). Children's initial encounters with print, N.I.E. Grant proposal. In V. H. Hardt (Ed.), *Teaching reading with the other language arts.* Newark, DE: International Reading Association, p. 44.

Conclusion (continued)

Juel, C. (1992). Longitudinal research on learning to read and write with at-risk students. In M. J. Dreher & W. H. Slater (Eds.). *Elementary school literacy: Critical issues* (pp. 73-99). Norwood, MA: Christopher-Gordon Publishers, Inc.

Meier, D. (1995). *The power of their ideas: Lessons for America from a small school in Harlem*. Boston, MA: Beacon Press.

Myers, Miles. (1996). *Changing our minds: Negotiating English and literacy*. Urbana, IL: National Council of Teachers of English.

Putnam, L. R. (1994, September). Reading instruction: What do we know that we didn't know thirty years ago? *Language Arts, 71,* 362-366.

Rosenholtz, W. (1989). *Teachers' workplace: The social organization of schools*. New York, New York: Longman.

Routman, R. (1996). *Literacy at the crossroads: Critical talk about reading, writing, and other teaching dilemmas*. Portsmouth, NH: Heinemann.

Sharp, D. L. M., Bransford, N. V., Goldman, S. R., Kinzer, C., & Soraci, S., Jr. (1992). Literacy in an age of integrated-media. In M. J. Dreher & W. H. Slater (Eds.), *Elementary school literacy: Critical issues* (pp. 183-210). Norwood, MA: Christopher-Gordon Publishers, Inc.

Smith, F. (1973). Twelve easy ways to make learning to read difficult. In F. Smith (Ed.), *Psycholinguistics and reading*. New York, NY: Holt, Rinehart, and Winston.

Yatvin, J. (1992, November). *Beginning a school literacy improvement project: Some words of advice*. Portland, OR: Northwest Regional Educational Laboratory.